A Sufi Master's Message

A Sufi Master's Message

Shaykh 'Abd al-Wahid Pallavicini

FONS VITAE

First published in 2010 by
Fons Vitae
49 Mockingbird Valley Drive
Louisville, KY 40207
http://www.fonsvitae.com
Email: fonsvitaeky@aol.com

Copyright Fons Vitae 2010

Library of Congress Control Number: 2010940859
ISBN 9781891785566

Printed in Canada

Table of Contents

Preface   7

Introduction   17

In Memoriam René Guénon   23

A Meeting of Genius and Holiness   31

"God Is Here"   37

Of the Beginning and of the End   47

Across the World's Center   57

APPENDIX Friday Sermon   67

In the Name of Allah, the Most Gracious, the Most Merciful

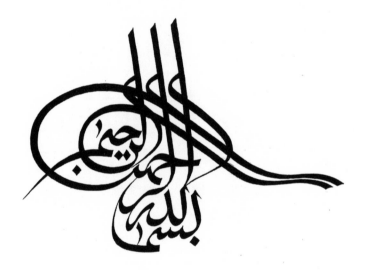

Preface

We believe that traditional Islam, which still exists today, is the true antidote to the ideological and radical tendencies currently exploiting religion.

We do not suggest, however, as many presume to do, a miracle cure for contemporary ideological exploitation of religion for political purposes. This disease of our time is not inherent to Islam but is endemic to our present era. The solution calls us to firmly grasp the "cord of Tradition" through Islamic orthodoxy. It appears that a certain mentality persists, even among Muslims (be they of the East or the West), which generates the tendency to fall into particular ideological trends designed to produce what has been termed the "clash of civilizations" and forms of totalitarianism.

At this critical moment in Islamic history, we would like to re-present reflections arising from the intellectual force of the doctrinal insight and metaphysical clarification of Shaykh 'Abd al-Wahid Yahya René Guénon. Through the collected writings of Shaykh Pallavicini, the president and founder of COREIS (*Comunità Religiosa Islamica,* the Italian Islamic Religious Community), we hope to spread the wisdom underlying Islamic orthodoxy to a wider audience.

Shaykh 'Abd al-Wahid Pallavicini's spiritual practice and metaphysical orientation gave him the resolve to return to Italy and bring home the blessings he received in the East. Upon his initial return, Italy in the seventies and eighties was a stranger to Islam; the country had yet to experience its current level of Muslim immigration. After having been totally unknown for many years, the shaykh's orientation has become well received in Italy.

During those decades, Shaykh 'Abd al-Wahid Pallavicini would meet with the ambassadors of Islamic countries for Friday prayers (*jumu'ah*). Oftentimes they were unable to gather even the minimum number of seven men needed to perform the ritual properly. As he worked to serve the first generation of Italian Muslims, the Shaykh contributed to the establishment of the Islamic Cultural Center of Italy that now manages the Great

Mosque of Rome. At that time, the refined and visionary Persian prince Abolghassem Amini was the Secretary General of the Islamic Center and he exerted great effort in establishing the Cultural Center and the Great Mosque of Rome. Despite being the largest in Europe, the mosque's ability to establish Islamic dialogue in Italy's capital, host to the seat of the Vatican, has since been diminished by power struggles and ideological influences both internal and external to the mosque.

Shaykh 'Abd al-Wahid Pallavicini, however, has functioned as an intermediary between Christianity and Islam since 1986 when he was in Assisi as one of the members of the Muslim delegation invited by Pope John Paul II to participate in the first meeting with the representatives of the world religions. He continued to bridge the two faiths during the years he acted as an ambassador between the Mosque of Rome and the Vatican. He channeled a metaphysical quality still present in both the Muslim and Christian Orthodox communities of the East. Abiding by the teachings of Shaykh 'Abd al-Wahid Yahya Guénon, he did not intend to bring the metaphysical message to Christianity itself—which has always had this perspective and always will—but rather to the institutional structure of Catholicism.

As a young man, he was already so well versed in Guénon's teachings that he was inspired to seek out Julius Evola, editor of the Italian translations of Guénon's books. In 1946 in Rome, Evola understood the Shaykh's search to be purely spiritual rather than political and pointed him in the direction of Titus Burkhardt; Evola and Burkhardt had been in correspondence before the war.

Titus Burkhardt, known by the Muslim name Ibrahim, lived in Bern and was among the first Europeans to convert to Islam because of the works of René Guénon. On January 7th, 1951, at the age of twenty-five, Shaykh 'Abd al-Wahid Pallavicini came to Islam at the hands of Sidi Ibrahim himself. Sidi Ibrahim Burkhardt gave him the name 'Abd al-Wahid, Servant of the Only One, as a tribute to 'Abd al-Wahid Yahya René Guénon, whose writings, Burkhardt could see, had inspired Shaykh Pallavicini's conversion to Islam. Only later did the Shaykh come to know that René Guénon had passed away in Cairo on the exact same day as his conversion.

This sign was clearly a reminder that the inheritance of a

8

standard Islamic name could become associated with a spiritual legacy whereby the faithful continuation and implementation of Guénon's work would be embodied. This was not a "succession," a term which Guénon never recognized in those who arbitrarily used it, but an entrance into the current of wisdom that had guided the great French metaphysician. Hence, carried along by this same current, Shaykh 'Abd al-Wahid Pallavicini entered the Alawiyah, an Islamic brotherhood with a branch in Lausanne, through one of its European representatives who had corresponded with Guénon.

In the twenty years that followed, Shaykh 'Abd al-Wahid Pallavicini lived in the East, where he embraced the opportunity to meet with what was perhaps the last generation of masters of Islamic esotericism (*tasawwuf*). He sought out masters such as Sami Effendi of the Naqshbandi Sufi order (*tariqah*) in Istanbul and Shaykh Hashimi of the Qadiriyah in Jerusalem.

His spiritual search, spanning from Morocco to Japan, finally brought him to Singapore, where he met Shaykh Hajj 'Abd ar-Rashid al-Linki (1918-92) of the Ahmadiyah-Idrissiyah-Shadhiliyah brotherhood. This particular order was founded by Shaykh Ahmad ibn Idris (b. Maysur 1750; d. Yemen 1837)[1] and is a branch of the ancient brotherhood of Shaykh Abu'l- Hasan ash-Shadhili (1196–1258). Shaykh Pallavicini's frequenting of this brotherhood led Shaykh Hajj 'Abd-ar-Rashid al-Linki to entrust him with the unexpected and unsought authorization (*ijazah*) to autonomously pass on spiritual influence and to initiate believers in the West.

The transfer of spiritual influence, however, remains in a completely different realm than that of conveying ideas through a book. Shaykh 'Abd al-Wahid Pallavicini has said,

> Too often, one has the impression that both writer and reader have only an informational intention and that, from their given individual positions, they limit themselves to acting as passive spectators in a story that is told or lived out on the stage of a theatre and in which they cannot, or will not, take part in anyway. This is not a matter of

---

1. Maysur is a suburb of the Moroccan Atlantic port of al-'Ara'ish, known as Larache. In addition to 1750 CE, the date of 1760 is also given for the year of Shaykh Ahmad ibn Idris' birth (Rex S. O'Fahey, *Enigmatic Saint: Ahmad ibn Idris and the Idrisi Tradition* [Evanston: Northwestern University Press, 1990], pp. 30-32).

"getting some culture," as we say today, or of choosing something to store up in the brain before moving on to something else; it is a question of becoming open to a reading that can have an effective resonance in our lives, especially in our inner lives; the inner life being the same in all religions, and spirituality being present in all men. It is to this end that we present a book that would otherwise have no *raison d'être*.[2]

Exactly whose message is being passed on through this book? Certainly that of the author, Shaykh 'Abd al-Wahid Pallavicini, who legitimately received this role of messenger. But Shaykh 'Abd al-Wahid Yahya René Guénon was his inspiration, and he in turn had other teachers whose knowledge naturally originated with the first of all masters, the Prophet Muhammad, the source of Islamic orthodoxy. All the true masters of Islam pass the same message to their followers: a living knowledge that, through faith, rituals, and virtue, truly transforms its recipient.

These links from a traditional chain confirm that the scope of this book's content derives not from the life and personal experience of a few individuals, but rather from the expression of a school of wisdom rooted in the contemplative dimension of Islam referred to as Sufism (*tasawwuf*).

It is worth remembering that every contemplative path aims solely to attain knowledge of God, a knowledge that enlightens us to our status as servants before the one and only Lord. The great Muslim saint Shaykh Ahmad ibn Idris (d. 1837) taught that there are three sources for this knowledge: the Holy Qur'an, the Prophetic *sunnah,* and *la adri* (I do not know).[3] One must ac-

---

2. Abd al-Wahid Pallavicini, *Islam interiore. La ricerca della Verità nella religione islamica* (Milano: Il Saggiatore, 2002), p.25.

3. Cited by Shaykh Ahmad ibn Idris in his treatise, "Refutation of the Adherence of Individual Opinion," *The Exoteric Ahmad ibn Idrîs: A Sufi's Critique of the Madhâhib and the Wahhâbîs*: *Four Arabic Texts with Translation and Commentary* by Bernard Radtke, John O'Kane, Knut S. Vikor, and R. S. O'Fahey (Leiden: Brill, 2000), 51, 99. Although on occasion referred to as a *hadith* of the Prophet, this report originally appears to be a saying of one of the Prophet's companions (*sahaba*), 'Abdullah ibn 'Umar. Among its subsequent transmitters was Imam Malik ibn Anas. It begins *"Al-'ilm thalatha..."* (Al-Khatib al-Baghdadi, *Ta'rikh Baghdad,* [Beirut: Dar al-Kutub al-'Ilmiya, nd], v. 4, p. 23.) Among the many traditional authors to cite it, Imam al-Ghazali noted it in his *Ihya 'ulum al-din* (Beirut: Dar al-Ma'rifa, 1982), v. 1, p. 69.

knowledge that one does *not know* before one can recognize that God alone is the Truth (*Huwa al-Haqq*).

The believer never seeks "outward signs" because everything has ambiguous meaning if approached by means of conventional linear logic. The traveler on the contemplative path looks only for Knowledge; and this Knowledge, when attained, is completely independent of the circumstances that served as its base. The circumstances should be understood in the light of Knowledge itself. The proper traditional method does not appeal to linear reasoning, which is necessarily outside the scope of spiritual realization. Instead it operates well beyond the limits of human beings, leading them to places they could not previously imagine. There is, however, a fundamental difference between those who passively submit to Divine Will and those who aspire to active and willing collaboration.

The key to active collaboration lies in the "custodianship and transmission of the body of the Tradition" (*amana*, literally "the trust"), preserved from one cycle to another through its rejuvenation by the saints and the *hunafâ* (communities of pure worshippers):

> From the Prophet Abraham until the last day, there will be men and women who will know how to practice their faith within the various religions with a spirit of concentration and dedication, of essentiality and generosity, of rigor and love, of discipline and authenticity. These men and women will be like the Prophet Abraham, *hanîfan muslimân*, a community of the faithful formed by spiritual authority. [...]
>
> The most useful model to follow, for those who maintain a metaphysical orientation and an eschatological perspective, corresponds to the model of the community of "pure worshippers in Spirit and Truth." This community consists of those who continue to pray and work in this world, preparing themselves for the next one, confident in God and the light of Prophecy and Holiness, which never ceases to enlighten the families of the elect; those who can accept their role and recognize in the effectiveness of their works the sign of an acceptance by God of their sacrifice.[4]

4. Yahya Pallavicini, *Dentro la Moschea* (Milano: BUR, 2007), 252.

The crisis of the modern world was analyzed with great subtlety and insight by Guénon, who recognized the unusual nature of the present age in its tendency to reverse the order of traditional and religious hierarchies. The vision of society as a collection of individuals and the illusion that everyone determines his or her own destiny deprives Reality of its vertical orientation towards God. Humanity thus assumes a single-dimension existence characterized by a version of history far removed from the concept of spiritual cycles present in Islam and other traditional civilizations.

In Islam, every cycle begins with a prophet and links naturally to the following cycle, beginning with Adam, the first man and the first prophet, and ending with Muhammad, the Seal of Prophecy. This is the primordial Tradition, unique among the numerous religions that derive from it. Called *ad-din al-qayyim* by Islam, the axial Tradition has been manifest since the beginning of Creation and will endure until the end of time, even though it goes largely unrecognized during certain periods of history.

Awareness of the one overarching Tradition cannot excuse one's lack of adherence to a single orthodox *religion*. Adherence to Tradition without the practice of orthodox religion gives rise to a multitude of modern "personal" or "natural" religions based on pantheism. Man's fall from grace has obscured the symbolic immediacy in which every sign of Creation refers back to its Creator. God revealed His Word by appointing some symbols above others, enabling Man to elevate himself toward Him. Religious rituals reflect this divine symbolic language. Their diligent practice gives the symbols new life and prevents them from becoming useless empty forms or vulnerable to exploitation.

Islamic tradition states that, at the end of time, "God will not withdraw all knowledge with an act that will take it away from all men, but will withdraw it by reducing the number of the wise until no more are left."[5] As René Guénon has admirably written, this passage refers to the presence of the spiritual elite who will ensure the Tradition's survival.

The contingent function of this elite—whose aim will always

---

5. *Sahih al-Bukhari*, ed. Mustafa Dib al-Bugha, *Kitab al-'Ilm, bab #34 Kayfa yuqbadu al-'ilm, hadith #100 Inna Allaha la yaqbidu al-'ilm...* (Damascus: al-Yamama, 1990), v. 1, p. 50; and ed. and trans. Muhammad Muhsin Khan (Dar al-Fikr, np., nd), v. 1, p. 80, *bab #35, hadith #100*.

remain spiritual realization—is to ensure a link between the East and West, and to impact the external world through adherence to pure intellectuality. They are the ark that ferries traditional heritage through the transition between the cycles, making the shift less dramatic.

This active function necessitates presence and concern for world events, yet simultaneously requires that they be detached from themselves as well as external events. This attitude is very different from that maintained by those who have withdrawn to the ivory tower of their own inner circle, believing themselves to be the only ones in the world able to maintain orientation toward the true Tradition through academic study.

We do not wish, however, to stir up the millenarian fears that have resurfaced today, mainly in America. Our only goal is to bear witness, in full Islamic orthodoxy, to the vigorous strength of the contemporary spiritual presence of the Prophet Muhammad. Prophetic presence will help Muslims face the end of time when, according to Islamic tradition, Sayyiduna 'Isa, Jesus, will return to judge whoever has been faithful to the spirit of the Tradition in each of its authentic manifestations.[6]

To forget this eschatological expectation and preach the indefinite progress of humanity reinforces the notion of an individualist "post-prophetic" period in which anyone may draw on elements from diverse traditions, much like choosing various books from a library. Today's world is a fertile breeding ground for these tendencies. Unfortunately the masses have a strong and growing fascination for pseudo-spirituality, allowing for the establishment of geographic and intellectual empires, or caliphates, through which they assert their own personal authority, rendering the authentic prophetic message nearly obsolete.

It is no coincidence that confusion about the relationship between spiritual authority and temporal power is used, more or less consciously, as an argument in all of today's geopolitical events to evoke a scenario of the final eschatological moments.

---

6. "Allah's Apostle said, 'By Him in Whose Hands my soul is, surely, (Jesus,) the son of Mary will soon descend amongst you and will judge mankind justly'" (*Sahih al-Bukhari,* ibid, *Kitab al-Buyu',* bab #102 *Qatl al-khinzir, hadith* #2109, v. 2, p. 774; ed. and trans. M. M. Khan, ibid, v. 3, pp. 233-34, *bab* #104, *hadith* #425; and "No one among the People of the Book will not believe in him [i.e., Jesus] before dying; and on the Day of Resurrection, he will be a witness against them" [Qur'an 4:159]).

In truth, the governing of this world is entrusted to men of Tradition in ways that profoundly change depending on cyclical conditions. Although in the past it was normal for spiritual and temporal power to be united in the same person (as occurred in the first community of Medina around the Prophet Muhammad), progression of the cycle and the apparent departure from Traditional principles led temporal power to naturally come under more and more chaotic management. Finally, as Shaykh 'Abd al-Wahid Yahya Guénon teaches, it would take on the form of a truly reversed "order," from which it can be salvaged only by the final eschatological events. Until that point, it will be more prudent to cultivate a quest for Knowledge through faith and ritual practice than to look for ways to restore forms of power that no longer belong to this phase of the cycle.

Men of Tradition should be marked by the greatest possible detachment, along with the greatest wariness of everything that opposes or inhibits following an orthodox path. They must be able to bear witness to those qualified to follow it. Tradition never ceases to pull the "cosmic wagon," even during phases that appear to be controlled by the "powers of illusion."

Authority, like Truth, asserts itself alone and, like a torch lighting another torch, is immediately recognized when it meets the right interlocutor. At present, one feels less the absence of men of Tradition in important positions than the lack of those who are spiritual centers. Such rare beacons may once again become points of reference that inspire people's actions in this world and serve as a *katechon*[7] against the outbreak of counter-traditional forces.[8]

Such exceptions to the perceived absence of true living spiritual authorities are perhaps best represented by one who, while possessed of a certain power, would maintain the discernment necessary to put this power in the service of the Truth. Such a leader should not be confused with one who allegedly possesses

7. The Katechon is the "wall" that prevents the manifestation of the Antichrist (see Paul, 2 Thessalonians 2:6-7). See also the *radm* ("wall") in Qur'an 18:94-100.

8. René Guénon makes the distinction between "anti-tradition," which is the negation of the spiritual vocation of human beings, and "counter-tradition," which is the rebellion and struggle against spirituality. See the last chapters of his book *Le règne de la quantité et les signes des temps* (*The Reign of Quantity and the Signs of the Times*).

14

knowledge and still strives to seize worldly power. Indeed, it may once again be possible for power to serve as a witness of truth, instead of truth being subservient to the conquest of power.

Despite everything, there are still present, even in the West, men who, by their 'interior constitution', are not 'modern men' but who are instead able to understand what the tradition essentially is and who do not agree to consider lay error as a *fait accompli*; it is only to such men that we have always wanted to turn.[9]

IlhamAllah Chiara Ferrero
Secretary General of COREIS
(Italian Islamic Religious Community)

---

9. René Guénon, *Initiation et Realisation Spirituelle* (Paris: Éditions tradition-nelles, 1952).

Shaykh Abd-al-Wahid Pallavicini
and his son Shaykh Yahya Pallavicini
in the Al-Wahid Mosque of Milan.

Introduction

A book dedicated to the memory of René Guénon necessarily contains the fundamental statement of his doctrine concerning the "Primordial Tradition." The "Universality of Abrahamic Monotheism," a concept referring to the religions that have come to predominate in the West, also reflects this doctrine.

Once we embrace universality, it is but a short step to the belief in one God for all mankind, a belief expressed in the Islamic statement of faith: "There is no god but Allah." *Allah* denotes precisely the Oneness of God; the One whose essential message René Guénon has so clearly pointed out in his works, and which is reflected in his Islamic name *'Abd al Wahid*, or the "servant of the One."

The path towards the realization of this truth lies in what Guénon calls "Metaphysics." This path goes beyond the boundaries of human individuality, giving rise to a transcendent Personality. Such transcendence is the source of the doctrines termed "metaphysical," which have their origin in that Orient to which metaphorically we must all be able to return, if not physically then, more importantly, in spirit.

This "Orient" serves as the inspiration for the statement that "God is here" in His immanence, even in the world where we search for the sole purpose of human life. Our purpose is to cultivate inner knowledge of God, renewed through the chain of revelations that have occurred up to the time of the last message. This knowledge is accessible through a continuing chain still present in Sufism, the living initiatory expression of the last revealed tradition, Islam.

It is this chain that allows correspondence and reconnection with a "Muslim saint of the twentieth century" and nourishes the hope of seeing a spiritual centre established in the West. This centre would offer men, in these latter days, a chance to radiate a sacredness that has been lost in the mists of time; a loss that is one of those "signs of the times" we are passing through in the imminence of an eschatology foreseen by all of the sacred texts.

It is said that at the end of time, the sun will no longer rise in the East, but will rise from the West. Forty years after Guénon's death, perhaps this prediction still holds promise. For the last prophetic message not only called itself "foreign born" but also prophesied that it will end as foreign: with what Guénon has taught us to call the "Primordial Tradition."

The Universality of Abrahamic Monotheism

At a time when words have lost meaning, and not just in an etymological sense, please forgive the pleonasm above: for "monotheism" should not have a different meaning than that of "universality," which etymologically refers "to the One," the one God of Abraham.

It is this Abrahamic origin that brings us closer to our Jewish brothers who did not want to close the Prophetic cycle with the coming of the Prophet Moses ('as), through whom the Word of God was made "Law." Through the continuation of this "Law," we Muslims, the last to arrive, were enabled to recognize the prophetic tidings in this final cycle of time, the Qur'an. This revelation was given to us by the last of the prophets: the *ummi*, literally "unlettered," Muhammad (s'aws).

The word "unlettered," referring to the Prophet Muhammad (s'aws), etymologically recalls not only the Islamic community (*ummah*) but also the word for "mother" (*umm*), the source of our existence. The "mother" figure also reminds us of the Virgin Mary, who in her immaculate innocence represents the "virgin" terrain in which God wrote his "Word," in the same way that He engraved in the heart of the Prophet the verses of our Holy Qur'an.[1]

Understanding our shared source of Prophecy in such terms enables us to include the figure of Sayyidna 'Isa ('as), Jesus Christ (regarded by Muslims as *Ruh Allah*, "Spirit of God"), in the prophetic succession, which thereby faithfully reflects the temporal succession of the Abrahamic monotheistic Revelations. We await the Second Coming of Sayyidna 'Isa ('as), along with our Christian brothers and sisters, as an "announcement of the Hour of the End," an eschatology also present in the Messianic expectation of our Jewish brothers and sisters.

It should be clearly understood that this "universalism," the fact that we are all directed towards the One God of Abraham, does not involve either syncretism or a mixture of traditional forms. Nor does it even involve relativism, because everything is effectively relative before the Absolute. Instead, "universality" requires the recognition of the equal personal dignity of a believer in any orthodox faith,

---

1. Yahya Pallavicini. La Sura di Maria. Traduzione e commento del capitolo XIX del Corano, (Brescia, Morcelliana 2010).

which, as such, necessarily entails the recognition of the salvific virtue of its dogmas, even though they may differ from each other.

To counter misleading views on syncretism and relativism, we took the liberty of sending a letter to the Pope on the occasion of his visit to the Synagogue of Rome in January 2010:

> Your Holiness, in Italy, where Islam has not been present for seven centuries, perhaps since the time of Frederick II, might an old Italian Muslim be allowed to feel some nostalgia for a unique period of history when the wise men of the three monotheistic revelations, from Maimonides to St. Albert the Great to Muhyiddin ibn 'Arabi, encouraged one another along the path to God within their respective faiths?
>
> Could not your august presence today at the Synagogue of Rome perhaps give us hope that, at least on an intellectual level, representatives of the different religions can still come together in this world that so needs an example of a return to holiness, in preparation for the Messiah's coming, for which we are all waiting, as proof of the sacrifice [*sacrum facere*, i.e., making sacred] that has led us to give a meaning to our life on this earth, where God has indeed brought us together?

Without wishing to stray too far from the topic proposed for this conference,[2] I would like to extend the concept of "victims of violence" beyond women to all religious men, in a world that seems to have forgotten the meaning of the sacred which, in the words of the First Letter of Saint Peter, made of us all "a nation of priests consecrated to God."

This concept is particularly important for us in Italy, where such a consecration seems reserved only for those who legitimately represent it as a member of a clergy, those specific to a single faith, excluding those belonging to other religions, who do not seem to have the right to such a sacredness even though they too were born in Italy.

On a personal note, I have just returned from a meeting with the Italian President Napolitano, where the King of Jordan was the guest of honour. "Do not judge by appearances," I said as I was wearing traditional Islamic clothes, "I'm Italian." "But God forbid,

---

2. Dublin, 5 June 2010. The 6th Religious Peace Conference "Science and Religion in the Age of the Unreasonable."

don't think about it," the President said, implying that an Italian can also be Muslim in Italy.

"But let not God forbid," I wanted to reply, "that there should be an official recognition of Islam as a religion." Italy is the only country in the world where Islam is not officially recognized as being equal to the other monotheistic faiths. But whenever we point out this absurdity to our non-Italian brother Muslims, they cannot imagine that such a situation is actually occurring. As is clear from some recent statements, Christianity today often seems to pretend to be a civil super-religion: by misinterpreting the proclaimed historic meeting with God on earth, there is the risk of forgetting the long-awaited return of the Messiah that we as Muslims must dutifully remind everyone about before it's too late.

We are, in fact, drawing near to an eschatological time, foreseen by all faiths, for which we must prepare ourselves and rediscover the meaning of our lives. God has asked us to make a choice of being either with Him or without Him, and if we stand with Him, then to accept the prophetic messages that have been passed on to us since the creation of mankind.

Islam is not the third revelation of Abrahamic Monotheism and this "Abrahamic" Monotheism does not go back to Abraham. There has always been "monotheism," even before Abraham, because God has never ceased to be "One" for all men on earth, or at least for those who have desired to obey Him.

This is the real sense of the word "Islam," which means submission to the One God, just as "Muslims" are literally all those who obey Him, even though they may be called "Jews" or "Christians," or even belong to one of the earlier orthodox religions.

"I was Prophet when Adam was still between water and clay," says the Prophet, which echoes the words of Jesus Christ: *"Before Abraham was, I am."* The immortal "Spirit of God," as we Muslims call Jesus, who instills in men the consciousness that they too have been made *"in the image and likeness of God,"* has been present since before the creation of the world.

It is precisely this likeness that allows men to be able to identify with the absolute Divine Presence through the rituals required by the various religions that have followed each other with the passing of time, rituals that renew the possibility of knowing that Knowledge which remains the only purpose of human life on this earth.

But what knowledge is this? The Knowledge of God! Because

"If God became man," as we are reminded by a saying of early Christianity still preserved in the doctrine of the Eastern Orthodox Church, it is in order to make *"man become God."* This occurs not through the affirmation of human individuality, but with the death of his egocentric nature that reflects also in the exclusivity of his choice of faith.

Naturally, some historical events may not exactly concur with those in other theologies, but the "Logos" that generated them is God Himself, who is above history; that is to say "meta-historical" just as He is "metaphysical." To paraphrase René Guénon, of whom I have the honour of sharing my Islamic first name, it is the "divine point of view" that is beyond all logic, even theological, in which the Logos is the vertical axis manifested according to the horizontal axes of time and place, which together represent the dimensions of the symbolism of the Cross.

In referring to this same symbolism, we would like to consider the Orthodox cross which, in its representation of the truth as present in each revealed revelation, and therefore "relative," has not two but three dimensions. It adds to the dimensions of length and width that of height, or rather "depth," so recalling the *"Pax profunda,"* or "Great Peace," which a "Sufi Saint of the Twentieth Century" would wish for whoever still desired, in these latter days, to understand the meaning of the "third dimension," a dimension equally present in the universality of Abrahamic monotheism.

Acknowledgments

The Author would like to express his profound gratitude to the following persons who have helped to make this book possible: H.R.H. Prince Ghazi bin Muhammad bin Talal for his kind presentation, Sidi Abd-al-Haqq Ismail Guiderdoni for his contribution of the "Friday Sermon" in the Appendix, IlhamAllah Chiara Ferrero for her preface and Prof. Alan Godlas for his patient editing of the English version of the text.

Shaykh 'Abd-al-Wahid Yahya René Guénon in Cairo

In Memoriam René Guénon[1]

Thirty years after the death of Shaykh 'Abd al-Wahid Yahya Guénon, we believe it necessary to dissipate some doctrinal misunderstandings seemingly elucidated by his works. These misunderstandings seem to be recurring, especially during attempts to apply the theoretical or "speculative" teachings in a practical or "operational" manner. Simultaneously, we find it necessary to denounce the recurring anti-traditional concepts that receive support from some exoteric and esoteric official authorities, not only in the West but also in the East.

Above all, let us not forget that our final and only aim is Knowledge (which can only be achieved through spiritual fulfillment); and that one must read the works of Guénon[2] in order to fully understand the meaning of such terms. Knowledge is not an encyclopedia of traditional notions; spiritual fulfillment is not merely the result of initiation into a doctrine. In addition, initiation is not an end where doctrinal knowledge is immediately and miraculously acquired, but rather, as the word itself indicates, it is an "initial" step in a process of lifelong purification. The outcome of the process depends not on the individual but on Divine Will. Nonetheless, initiation is essential in order to receive a certain esotericism's spiritual influence and tools, both of which establish the necessary foundation for the desired outcome.

Obviously initiation requires esotericism because initiation implies entry into an esoteric order. At the same time, no esoteric order or esotericism can exist without an exoteric form. Under different historical conditions there existed, and continue to exist, non-religious exoteric

---

1. Translation of the eponymous French text in the pamphlet published by Arché, Milan, 1981.

2. In particular, we suggest to novices the following works of Guénon: for the critic of the modern world and the description of the traditional civilizations see "La Crise du monde moderne" (Paris: Gallimard, 1994), "Orient et Occident" (Paris: Trédaniel, 1993) and "Le Règne de la quantité et les signes des temps" (Paris: Gallimard, 1994); for a brief introduction to the doctrine of Knowledge see "La Métaphysique orientale" (Paris: Ed. traditionnelles, 1993), and a thorough development "Le Symbolisme de la croix" (Paris: Trédaniel, 1996) and "Symboles de la science sacrée" (Paris: Gallimard, 1962); finally the necessity of religious practices and the specificity of esotericism are described in "Aperçus sur l'initiation" (Paris: Ed. Traditionnelles, 1992) and "Initiation et réalisation spirituelle" (Paris: Ed. traditionnelles, 1990).

organizations; however, it is obvious that, for us Westerners today, exotericism necessarily means a religion.

This is providential. If men were closer to the primordial Tradition, either in time or by virtue of their integrity, they would have no need of an exoteric religion. In the modern West, exoteric forms best suit our religious practice due to our level of decadence. Our ability to imagine the state of primordial men and to intellectually anticipate our "re-integration" into that state barely changes our human need for the support that religion offers.

Belonging to a particular religion is therefore not only a formal *conditio sine qua non* of initiation to the corresponding esotericism, but is also a necessary and natural qualification. Adhering to all the modalities of a particular religion, be they concerned with virtue or faith, produces the fertile ground in which the seed of initiation germinates. By requiring a certain degree of preparation, this dynamic avoids both the dispersion of, and the deviation from, real esotericism.

It is not just a question of belonging to a religion in the literal sense —by learning its "sacred language," "theological doctrine," and "ritual technique." Above all, it is about learning to live the "spirit" and becoming truly "religious." True religiosity requires us to abandon our non-religious independence and accept a dependence upon the Principle to which, as can be seen from the etymology of the word "religion," we are "reconnecting," *both* exoterically *and* esoterically.

Such partnership is the essential difference between the sacred and the profane; alleged methods of esoteric achievement that neglect adherence to religion for contingent or factual reasons appear "sinister" and will always be a "desecration." What results can one expect when he or she fails to follow God-given laws, or even those of "nature"? And what holiness can one approach with hypocrisy and dishonesty, vanity and envy, arrogance and wickedness, immorality or amorality? What kind of enlightenment would that be? Perhaps that of an "absolute individual" no longer seen as synonymous with the Self, but on the contrary, as a hypertrophy of the "ego." We know that "as long as we are, He is not." Have we not yet understood that we must "contain ourselves" in a form of religion that brings us to a theocentric dimension? And that only by starting from the center of our individuality can we aspire to realize a Personality that transcends us?

For example, what would happen if we pursued a profane path, one without the exoteric dimension of religion, and arriving at a practical plan, we relegated the significance of certain concepts—sacrificing the

24

ego, knowing how to die before dying, and worshipping God, Allah, as if we saw Him, because even if we do not see Him, He sees us—to the purely theoretical? Such an approach is like trying to raise oneself up by oneself, like someone pulling himself up by the hair. A practice so intensely presumptuous in doctrine and technical rigor neglects the sincerity of our intentions; we become consummate social climbers that attempt to deceive God and only deceive ourselves.

The same "desecration," understood metaphorically here as meaning "to stay outside the temple," traces back to the by-products of traditional life that seem to seduce anyone who, "descending" from the domain of pure metaphysics to that of ritual practice, discovers that his real interest was only in studying the *possibility* of achieving spiritual enlightenment more than enlightenment itself. Unable to detach from the intellectual complacency of the past for what seems to be a "leap in the dark," one tries to color his or her "ordinary life" with proselytizing, political-interventionism, or eschatological utopias. If we cannot prevent some people from pursuing such ends, then at least we can deter them from involving others in the descent.

A number of purveyors of a certain pseudo-Islamic decadence expect to preach this incomplete practice in the West, especially to Western converts to Islam. Such a message creates difficulties for "Guénonian" converts to Islam, difficulties mainly arising from the fact that, from the perspective of some born Muslims, any conversion to Islam should imply a repudiation of Christian beliefs. Their repudiation, in the best cases, denies Christianity's validity in its esoteric and exoteric forms because of its pre-Islamic origin, despite the completely opposing statements of the Qur'an itself.[3] These ideas not only concern pre-Islamic religious practice in general, which may still be somewhat acceptable, but also the principles of those religions. For these Muslims, those who do not recognize the coming of the Prophet, however orthodox, are considered non-believers. Even those Muslims adhering to Islam and its Law are labeled non-believers if they embrace the current validity of the messages of the preceding prophets (not to mention the traditions

---

3. "To each of us we have granted a Law and a Way. If God had wanted, He would have made of you one community, but this He did not do, to test you in what was given to you. Make competition, therefore, with good works, which all return to God, and then He will inform you about those things for which you are now in disagreement (Qur'an 5:48)." "Indeed, those who believe, those who practice Judaism, Christians, and Sabaeans—whoever believes in God and the Last Day, and acts with righteousness—they will have their reward in the presence of their Lord; and neither will fear be upon them, nor will they grieve (Qur'an 2:62).

that are conceived in the strictest historical sense of the word as "non-Abrahamic").

The same exclusivity is also present on an esoteric level. For the Guénonian, there do not seem to be great differences among the various *turuq* (plural of *tariqah*, "a spiritual path or Sufi order"). But many born Muslims—who usually arrive at their own *turuq* not by vocation or affinity but by birth—tend to consider their own *turuq* as exclusive "groups" superior to all others. Such Muslims tend not to recognize "outsiders" as good believers, whether they belong to other *turuq*, other religions, or are their own Muslim brothers.

Therefore, particularly exclusive and misguided *turuq*, or at least some of their places of worship (Ar., *zawaya'*) that once were legitimate centers for the propagation of Islam or the independence of some Islamic countries, have today become the (more or less conscious) tools of deviant activists and militant movements. Similar deviations from principle were present in the practices of certain Catholic missionaries that fulfilled expansionist and political aims during the times of European colonialism. Such a misguided practice represents a type of reversed anachronistic crusade that has become, if not the principle, then the mask of the real Islam.

Today's situation is aggravated by the economic and strategic importance of some Islamic countries and their corresponding self-styled "Islamic" organizations (divided and opposed by the usual capitalist or progressive, conservative or revolutionary trends). Those who invoke Islam in promotion of a superpower or "infra-power" have also exacerbated the loss of Islamic esotericism. People who tout the official and global return to Islamic fundamentalism unjustifiably valorize an idea of an Islam that has lost its awareness of the Spirit.

Thus it is not surprising that militant Islamic extremism, instigating "rebellion" and terrorism in order to establish a renowned caliphate or "empire" in Islamic countries and throughout the world, does not come from the East. Such a militant movement is, from the perspective of a certain élite, a twisted parody of the *tariqah* that René Guénon deigned a possible vehicle for salvation and spiritual fulfillment.

It should be clear that—aside from the limited cases of certain extremist fanatics who seem to have abandoned their own past, perhaps not because it was a Christian past so much as it was their own—the path to conversion is generally unrelated to a rejection of Christianity. Conversions usually stem from an acceptance of Islam, and an induction into the final expression of the primordial Tradition (*din al-qayyimah*,

Qur'an 98:5), a Tradition that embraces the truth of the Revelations preceding it (e.g., the Torah and the Gospels) and revives the possibility of spiritual realization through confirmation of antecedent messages. Nothing in the *shari'ah* (compilation of Islamic Law) could abrogate the Ten Commandments, nor could the Commandments constitute an obstacle to spiritual fulfillment. Such obstacles may instead be found in the decadence of certain exoteric organizations and in the inaccessibility of certain esoteric orders. These obstacles are consequences of rationalist and sentimental influences that are not original to Christianity, but are creations of the modern West.

If these rationalist and sentimental influences have in some way rendered unlikable the religion into which we were born, then there is a potentially reactionary tendency to associate these influences with that which we have tried to avoid. Although the logical and emotional aspects of every Tradition are integral to man and therefore comprise the necessary "material" for an alchemical mutation, we highlight the doctrinal and technical aspects instead. It is as if the works of René Guénon had automatically led us beyond our ontological limits, qualifying us for a titanic process of realization based almost exclusively on a technique exempt from any "human" participation and independent of all providential divine intervention.

If we have found the traditional truths in books, then to "fulfill" them we must find within ourselves certain "virtues" that may have withered and corrupted our behavior in turn. The "tests to pass" do not involve knowledge of Arabic, speed at reading the Qur'an, or the study of comparative religion. Instead they call for repentance (*tawbah*), effort (*jahd*), abandonment unto God (*tawakkul*), and most importantly, love of God (*mahabbah*). *Mahabbah* is also found in *tasawwuf* (Sufism), but its misinterpretation has distanced some from its practical aspects.

It is true that developing these virtues entails learning a technique, but the process is not physical. A physical process occurs when a piston produces a "breath" without altering its own mechanical components. The cultivation of virtue is akin to a "chemical," or rather alchemical, process, such as the reaction of hydrogen and oxygen that ends each component's gaseous state and produces water.

The process of fulfilling truths involves becoming something else. But to *become*, one must *be*, and to be one must *do*, and to do one must *know*, and to know one must *desire to know*. It is not enough to want, or to know, or to do, if one *is* not. In order to transform oneself, one must use all of his or her human "essence," including mental faculties (presence and concentration) and emotional aptitude (sincerity and devotion), in order to be receptive to that which transcends this "essence." It is in "passing through this process" that one is transformed, *insha'Allah* (God willing).

As the essential truths of the different traditions come together in our One God, so do the techniques of spiritual enlightenment come together in man. However, the similarities between these methods do not make them equivalent to each other; their corresponding forms of revelation are unique in that they each highlight a different aspect of the Truth. In addition, the structures that channel spiritual influence to a particular revelation are as specifically adapted to time and place as the revelation itself: they are not interchangeable.

Thus we cannot "Christianize" Islam, even from a methodological point of view. We cannot color our participation in *tasawwuf* with a Christian "mystical" attitude, such as an ascetic detachment from life and the world. Nor can we expect to build an Islamic monastic structure, even one inspired by hesychasm,[4] since Islam has neither monasticism nor clergy.

Finally, we cannot expect Islam to be the same as it was at the time of the Prophet because we cannot recreate the Middle Ages in today's modern world. Sufism, the esoteric essence of Islam, instead aims to reintegrate man into his primordial state where Islam is eternal and universal regardless of our living conditions, which have changed and continue to change over centuries and latitudes. True Islam allows one to live Islam's spirit and to follow its law wherever one may be and at any given point in time, even at the end of times. Indeed, the Sunnah identifies the end of times as the period when Islam will spread to new parts of the world.[5]

Therefore we should not form Islamic communities detached from the rest of humanity because they may serve to support anachronistic restorations or political influences like those troubling Europe. Likewise, it would not be considered Islamic in the Sufi methodology to reject the concomitance necessary for life experience by refusing responsibility towards family and work. Regardless of personal characteristics

---

4. Hesychasm is an Eastern Orthodox tradition involving contemplation and retreat.

5. At the end of times, "Islam will spread throughout the earth…" (*wa-yulqi al-islam bi-jiranih fi l-ard*) (Abu Da'ud, *Sunan, kitab al-mahdi,* (Cairo: Mustafa al-Babi al-Halabi, 1983), v. 2, p. 461, beginning "*Yakunu ikhtilaf 'inda mawt khalifa…*" and Tabarani, *al-Mu'jam al-awsat,* ed. Mahmud Tahhan (Riyadh: Maktabat al-Ma'arif, 1986), v. 2, pp. 89-90, *hadith* #1175).

and aspirations, acceptance of Islam represents a major adherence to the reality known as the expression of the Divine Will.

In this sense, we do not reject life or the world in itself, but instead denounce the parts of the modern world that are anti-traditional and thus inhibit our spiritual development. We children of the modern West are still profane, but we can overcome anti-traditional obstacles by way of an inner transformation that is in fact the aim of our conversion and ensuing spiritual vocations. The obstacles then become the support for our fulfillment. We want to escape the difficulties of life that all men face and seek refuge in the ivory tower of tradition, full of elective affinities and pleasing habits; nevertheless, we neither refuse human duty nor make our traditional interest the core of our activities.

Within *tasawwuf* (Sufism) is the measure of our life and certainly not the measure of its evasion. Sufism does not save us from lack of understanding or human feelings, nor can it substitute for the satisfaction of professional or social life. It cannot serve as a "profession" or a "career" in which to find the means for personal expression or survival.

Many spiritual masters and/or teachers in the East are heads of families that carry out a "profane" profession, if one categorizes the medical, judicial, military, or administrative professions as such. The majority of their disciples are not academically concerned with *tasawwuf* but rather practice it in the same way that Muslims go to mosques to pray and do not concern themselves more deeply with talk about Islam. Outside the mosque, they live as good Muslims, even in the company of non-believers, and even if working in profane professions.

The Dalai Lama addressed the heads of the Tibetan monasteries that were destroyed during the 1949 Chinese invasion. The book *Born in Tibet*[6] documents his speech, the sense of which follows: "It seems that the times of teaching through monastic orders has passed; it may now be time to return to the oral and secret teachings that will save us from the persecutions dealt with until now."

One day an envoy of the Algerian government, aware of Shaykh al-Alawi's power, proposed a collaboration with the government that would have closed down all the places of worship (*zuwaya'*) of the other *turuq*. To that offer the Shaykh replied: "It would be better if the government closed my *zawiya* and left the others open, because they need to exist, whereas my *fuqara'* (disciples) carry the *zawiya* in their hearts."

---

6. Chögyam Trungpa, *Born in Tibet* (Boston: Shambala, 1985).

Shaykh Abu al-Abbas Ahmad ibn Mustafa
al-'Alawi. Mostaghanem 1905.

A Meeting of Genius and Holiness[1]

The connection between René Guénon and Shaykh Ahmad al-Alawi is far from arbitrary. Although they never met in person, these two contemporaries communicated between Mostaghanem and Cairo. Though we know almost nothing of their epistolary relationship, we can easily observe the impact they both had, not only on their countrymen or those who met them personally during their lives, but also on those indirectly benefiting from their teachings.

Shaykh al-Alawi (1869–1934) was the founder of the *tariqah* that bears his name. The Alawiyah (not to be confused with the Alawite Syrian sect) derives from the Darqawiyah *tariqah* to which the Shaykh belonged. The Darqawiyah was itself a derivation of the Shadhiliyah *tariqah* to which René Guénon ('Abd al-Wahid Yahya) was connected after his adherence to Islam.

René Guénon dedicated *The Symbolism of the Cross*, one of his most important works, to the memory of his own teacher, Shaykh 'Abd al-Rahman 'Allish al-Kabir, adding that the book's inspiration came from him. His reasoning is laid clear in a passage from the introduction of this book:

> We have said that the cross is one of the symbols that, in different forms, can be found almost everywhere since the most remote times; therefore, it is far from belonging exclusively to Christianity, as some may believe. Christianity itself seems to have, at least in its more well-known exterior aspect, lost sight of the symbolic meaning of the cross, considering it to be merely a tangible symbol of a historic event. These two points of view, [however], are not mutually exclusive; in fact, the second is, in a way, a consequence of the first; but this is so foreign to the mentality of the greater part of our contemporaries that, in order to avoid misunderstandings, it is better to linger on the subject for a while.
>
> Too often one is led to think that the admission of a symbolic sense [of things] implies the exclusion of the literal or

---

1. Translation of the eponymous chapter from 'Abd al-Wahid Pallavicini, *Islam interiore, la spiritualità universale nella religione islamica* (Milan: Mondadori, series Uomini e Religioni, 1991).

historic sense: such an opinion is nothing but the result of the ignorance of the law of correspondence that is actually the foundation of all symbolism. By virtue of this law, anything (which as such proceeds from a metaphysical principle on which its reality solely depends) translates or expresses [that principle]—in its own way and according to its order of existence—so that from one order to the other, all things are linked and correspond to one another, participating in a total and universal harmony that, in the multiplicity of manifestation, is like a reflection of the principal Unity.[2]

Here we have, in the unmistakable style of the man known as the "Unifier" (a quality suggested by his Arabic name 'Abd al-Wahid, "servant of the One"), a clear affirmation of the Islamic doctrine of *tawhid*,[3] the doctrine of Unity. He presents the concept of a Principle from which all is derived and to which we can only refer in the hope of finding within ourselves, and in relation to others, the sense of "universal harmony." It is precisely this sense of unity that we in both in the East and the West have distanced ourselves from today.

On the other hand, Shaykh Ahmad al-Alawi was connected to the Isawiyah *tariqah*, or "Jesuitic path," and he is considered a saint of the "Isawa" or "Christ" type. Within the Shadhili-Darqawi derivation, he represents an expression of Islam's revival that began in the nineteenth century with two other great Ahmads of the Maghrib: Shaykh Ahmad Tijani (1735–1815) and Shaykh Ahmad ibn Idris (1760–1837). Doctor Marcel Carret visited and treated Shaykh al-Alawi during the last years of his life. He described the Shaykh:

> The first thing that struck me was his likeness to the usual representations of Christ. His clothes, so nearly if not exactly the same as those which Jesus must have worn, the fine lawn[4]

---

2. René Guénon, *Le Symbolisme de la Croix* (Paris, 1932); see *The Symbolism of the Cross*, translated by Angus Macnab (London: Luzac & Company), pp. xi-xii.

3. From the religious point of view, *tawhid* derives from *al-Wahid*, or the One, one of the 99 divine names, indicating Oneness, correspond to recognizing the testimony of the divine Unity; this is expressed by the first part of the *shahadah*, which states: "There is no god but God." Metaphysically, *Tawhid* can be used as "Knowledge of the Oneness" or, as it is often used in the language of Sufism, "the realization of the Oneness," of that Unity that constitutes the interior and essential heritage of any tradition, a unity not conditioned by the multiplicity of its outward manifestations.

4. "Lawn" is "a sort of fine linen or cambric; extended to some cottons" (Chambers 20th Century Dictionary, [1983] s.v. "lawn").

head cloth which framed his face, his whole attitude—everything conspired to reinforce the likeness. It occurred to me that such must have been the appearance of Christ when he received his disciples at the time when he was staying with Martha and Mary.[5]

Clearly such relationships, understood in the words and works of René Guénon, do not seek to encourage either a kinship that forgets the principles of every religious faith or a useless doctrinal syncretism. Rather, they are an invitation to see and understand unity in multiplicity, and to recognize the validity of each revealed expression as a manifested and differentiated aspect of Truth. Truth, like Allah, is one and the same for all.

René Guénon's so-called conversion from Christianity to Islam should not be misunderstood as a rejection of his original religion. Instead, it should be regarded as an acceptance of Islam through which he joined what he called the Primordial Tradition (*din al-qayimah*) in its final expression, which incorporates all previous Revelations without opposing them.

This is not a matter of searching for compromise or a common denominator among the various doctrinal positions of our religions. It is a matter of reconstructing the eroded integrity of believers until our communities resemble those that existed during the prophetic moments characterizing each religion's historic origin. Today, the various ethnic groups constituting the support base of each respective revelation have, in many cases, developed the worst aspects of their temperaments to the detriment of their spirituality. In the West, intellectuality has become intellectualism and logic has become rationalism or, worse still, psychologism; in the East, intuition has created impulsiveness and fatalism has produced fanaticism.

We need an exchange in which believers, from both the West and East, learn how to regenerate the beneficial waves of their complementary attributes from the respective shores of their common sea. In this way, we Westerners will return to intelligence, regaining our divinity by reflecting upon the intellect of God. Likewise, the East will once again manifest His Light when the Easterner rediscovers his or her own innate sense of divine immanence.

Shaykh al-Alawi used to answer his French doctor who believed

---

5. Martin Lings, *A Moslem Saint of the Twentieth Century: Shaikh Ahmad al-Alawi* (London: George Allen & Unwin Ltd, 1961), p. 14.

that all beliefs are equal:

> They are all equal if you only consider the question of being set at rest. But there are different degrees. Some people are set at rest by very little; others find their satisfaction in religion; some require more; it is not only peace of mind that they must have, but the Great Peace, which brings with it the plenitude of the Spirit. "What about religion?" persisted the doctor. "For these last," answered the Shaykh, "religion is only a starting point, above religion there is doctrine, the means of attaining to God Himself, but why should I tell you, since you are not disposed to make use of them? If you came to me as my disciple I could give you an answer. But what would be the good of satisfying an idle curiosity? Do you know what is lacking in you? To be one of us and to see the Truth, you lack the desire to raise your Spirit above yourself. And that is irremediable."[6]

René Guénon, hoping to reawaken the concept of a transcendent reality, attempted to resolve the lack of spirit in modern Westerners by speaking to them in a manner matching their ability to understand.[7] The yearning for spiritual realization, or gnosis, is a yearning for Knowledge attainable only through one's reinsertion into an established Tradition, accompanied by the rediscovery of spiritual values *and* fundamental human virtues. Guénon himself, in the introduction to his *The Crisis of the Modern World*, expressed these goals in the following manner:

> All we can undertake at the moment is to contribute, to a certain extent and as far as the means at our disposal allow, toward making aware those capable of it, of some of the consequences that seem already fully established. By so doing we shall be preparing the ground, albeit in a partial and rather indirect manner, for those who must play their part in the future 'judgment,' following which a new era will open in the history of mankind.[8]

René Guénon recognized, in our times, the signs of the end of a specific

---

6. Lings, ibid, p. 28

7. "Grant me honourable mention on the tongue of truth among the latest (generations)," Qur'an 24:84.

8. René Guénon, *The Crisis of the Modern World*, translated by Arthur Osborne, Marco Pallis, and Richard C. Nicholson (London: Luzac & Company, 1962), p. 3.

cycle predicted by all the sacred texts. He hoped for the establishment in the West of a *tariqah*, a brotherhood possessing an autonomous and esoteric quality. This same quality allowed Christian organizations to exist during the Inquisition, a religious period paralleling contemporary Islam in decadence. The inevitability of decadence characterizes a destiny common to all religions. According to Shaykh 'Abd al-Wahid Yahya Guénon, some seeds of Knowledge will remain intact at the "end of time," or the period signifying the end of *a* world.

After clearing the ground of such weeds as occultisms and spiritualisms still spreading at the start of the last century, René Guénon began to battle the prejudices and false idols established by the modernist, evolutionist, and progressivist theories. Since the creation of Man, these same theories have impeded the majority from finding the faith and acceptance of spiritual reality present in the sacred texts.

His work aimed to help many find a path toward the Tradition of origin and he helped some (as in his own case) to find adherence to the Tradition of Islam that has concluded the cycle of Revelations in our time. This Tradition continues to offer the possibility of an initiatic reconnection today. Such concepts and connections caused Guénon to be attacked as a syncretist, an apostate, and an esotericist (in the magical or occultist sense of the word), attacks including attempts at denigration and a type of conspiracy against him. Now his detractors attempt to plagiarize and contort his works; unable to beat him, they decided to try to incorporate him and his work into their own agenda.

These forces, called "counter-tradition" by René Guénon, have become stronger now that people no longer believe in either God or the devil. "Counter tradition" is now free to spread its influence not only outside the structures of the various religious forms, but also within them. With the aid of false teachers, these negative forces seek to falsify the concept of the metaphysical equality of religions in order to create syncretic practices, not only in their ideology but also in their rituals.

Due to his universalism and his particular ability to validate the sacredness of other religious forms without detaching himself from Islamic orthodoxy, Shaykh al-Alawi was not insusceptible to attacks of vacuous criticism from the usual "doctors of law." One day, when reprimanded for the fact that his *tasbih* (prayer beads) resembled a cross, the Shaykh stood up, lifted and spread out his arms at shoulder height and exclaimed: "And what do we resemble?"

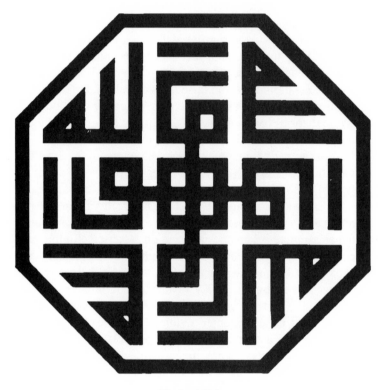

He is Allah

"God Is Here"[1]

What is most striking in these modern days, filled with billboards and radio commercials, is to see—in spray-paint or charcoal on a milestone or at a tunnel entrance—the statement, "God is here." Astonishment at this fact is motivated by two opposing feelings. One stems from our contemplative tendency, which might find it strange that, in broad daylight and under the vault of heaven, one would need to express in words what should be absolutely obvious for the spirit. The other feeling, however, arises from our critical spirit which causes us to appreciate, in today's world, the work of the unknown hand of somebody who can still bear witness, albeit with words, to the oldest and most essential Truth. These feelings indicate the boundaries between which modern Man is suspended. Even if he has lost transcendental experiences, he has not resigned to believing that the visible world is all that there is. Thus, Man remains like a fish out of water.

The first reaction brings to mind the story of a young fish that heard about the ocean. When he asked his parents if they knew where the ocean was, they responded that they had never heard of its whereabouts. Thus dissatisfied, the young fish left his family to travel the world far and wide, looking for someone who could tell him the location of the ocean. No one he encountered ever knew how to answer him, and, in the end, the poor fish died without finding the ocean. Perhaps a cuttlefish or a squid should have written the word "ocean" on a piece of seaweed or on a rock, so that our young fish might have realized that he was actually already immersed in it and that he himself constituted a small part of its whole.

Seeing "God is here" written on a stone is also reminiscent of the statement by a Buddhist Master according to which "Zen," the essence of his religion, was like "praying in a taxi." His central point consisted in sacralizing even the most profane moments and places of our existence, a practice true to the original meaning of the word "sacralize," which is "sacrifice" (L., *sacrum facere*). In the same

---

1. Translation of the eponymous chapter in French from 'Abd al-Wahid Pallavicini, *L'Islam Intérieur*, (Paris: Christian De Bartillat, 1995) and in Italian in Yahya Pallavicini, ed. *Dentro la Moschea* (*Inside the Mosque*) (Milan: B.U.R. Rizzoli Universal Library, 2007).

vein, "existence" comes from the Latin *ex-sistere*, to "stay outside," like a fish out of water or like a fish ignorant of the ocean's location. To exist, therefore, is not to *be*, because God alone *is*. The word "religion," on the other hand, derives from the Latin *religio*, "to bind" (cf., as the pages of a book are gathered together), or rather, "to reconnect," in the way that Man connects once again with God. The only way for Man not to merely exist, but to *Be*, is through the thread that links his essence to his Creator and makes every moment of his life sacred.

"But how?" the student asked.

"By praying," said the Zen Master, "even in a taxi," meaning praying outside consecrated places or ritual moments. Certainly the Master referred to a ritual prayer, not an individual extemporary prayer. Only a religious rite can reconnect us to the source of spirituality from which it originates, thus allowing us to drink of the purifying force channeled toward the part of ourselves that transcends our individuality.

In a world like ours, obsessed by magnetic powers and subtle influences, it is truly strange that religion is regarded as something strictly psychological, and that it is denied any dependence on its true value: spiritual blessings. This happens because Man today has lost his sense of transcendence and thus remains open to all sorts of psychological influences no longer balanced by spiritual ones. Of the Medieval ternary *spiritus, anima,* and *corpus,* only a body and a confused soul remain. Today's Man tends to consider only logic and rationality to be right and true; and, instead of making the profane moments of his life sacred, he refuses even to participate in the strictly ritual moments in the places consecrated to them.

The most common objection says: "Why go to church to pray when I can pray at home?" Such a perspective misunderstands the value of ritual prayer compared with individual prayer, as well as the need, indicated by God Himself, for ritually coming together at the right time and place, for His possible manifestation.[2] The other most common excuse for avoiding religious ritual involves judging those officiating the ritual as unworthy, and those participating as insincere, as if the worth of a ritual could ever be diminished by the individuality of the priest, or our fervor contaminated by the intentions of those around us. Certainly, "right intention" (incidentally, one of the eight rules of Buddhism) is a propitiatory element for the

2. See Qur'an 62:9.

effectiveness of a religious rite, operating by itself regardless of our awareness. However, it is also said that "the way to hell is paved with good intentions," especially when, instead of leading to practical action, they remain mere intentions.

Religion is, above all, action—ritual practice to which we have been led by understanding doctrine, belief, and faith. But belief is not enough to make one religious, just as it is not enough to "honor your neighbor" in order to avoid going to hell. Contemplating food or thinking about flowing water cannot be a substitute for eating and drinking. Likewise, our *spiritus* (a concept which was abandoned in the texts of the Middle Ages) requires that its nourishment comes exclusively from its own dimension and that no reasoning can ever replace this condition.

We do not intend to undervalue reason's (a gift reserved for Mankind to help us discover the Truth before we believe) ability to enable people to obey the Law that comes from a Revelation far beyond human reason. Usually we measure religious commands and prohibitions with the yardstick of our utilitarian logic. For example, some philosophers propose that Muslims are forbidden pork and alcohol for hygienic or climatic reasons. But God is neither a dietician nor a hygienist. The Prophets are primarily concerned not with the physical welfare of their followers, but with their sacralization. At the basis of all the laws and precepts of the various religions is the concept of "sacrifice," not merely as self-denial, but as "consecration."

The two most serious objections to religion stem from their profusion: the multiplicity of coexisting religions seems to be proof of their invalidity, and the fact that people fight in the name of religion seems to prove their ineffectiveness. Here again, principles have become confused with their manifestations, and religions have become confused with their representatives. Using a purely human judgment, namely rationalism, as a basis for analysis renders religions' founders the equivalent of spokesmen for philosophical systems of polemics (if not socio-political ideologies) or even visionary humanists. Such assessments ignore the qualities of the Prophets succeeding each other since the creation of Man.

Conflicts among followers of different religions (conflicts of which we speak so much today) or among adherents of the same religion are sometimes due to individualism and sometimes due to political manipulations of groups seeking power. At other times, servants of the spirit of that religion may even incite conflict. For example, Christ drove the money lenders from the Temple of Solomon, but he certainly did not break the tablets of the Law recognized by his disciples. And at the same moment that Muhammad destroyed the idols of the *Ka'bah*, he placed a protecting hand on the portrait of the Virgin and her son.

The monotheistic revelations—Judaism, Christianity, and Islam—recognize the prophet Abraham as their patriarch and traditionally acknowledge the validity of their predecessor religion(s). From a dogmatic point of view, these religions cannot entirely incorporate previous religions because they would risk losing their identity. Nonetheless, One is the God to whom they all refer and about whom they proclaim the absoluteness of Being. Within the great monotheistic tradition it is clear: God is here.

Returning to the Buddhist teacher, and understanding his advice to pray "even in a taxi" and at any time, rather than only in the temple at the canonical hours, we must emphasize that these are the words of a Zen Master. Clearly, there is no Zen without Buddhism, and although the inner or esoteric dimension of every religion necessarily has affinities with those of other religions, there is also no Yoga without Hinduism, no Kabbalism without Judaism, or Sufism without Islam, nor is there true Hesychasm (the last surviving form of Christian esoterism) outside the Orthodox Church.

In all of these cases, the relationship between these mystical traditions and their respective orthodoxies is unquestionable: they employ ritual practices beyond the purely religious or exoteric. However, they are characterized by their use of methods for channeling the spiritual influence passed on by the founder of an order or a brotherhood to their successors to facilitate spiritual enlightenment in sincere participants. The term "spiritual enlightenment" means the full awareness and possession of truths already accepted as dogma in our own respective religious creed. If well understood and well directed, initiatic practice can lead, God willing, to intellectual intuition.

The meaning of "initiation" should be cleared of prejudice and misunderstanding: initiation refers to one's entry into an esoteric brotherhood of a specific religion to which a person already belongs. He or she will continue to regularly observe the exoteric precepts and rituals of that religion, even after initiation.

The pretentiousness of "transcendental meditation," a practice divorced from all religious context, is simply the response of certain pseudo-masters to elitist sectarian and irresponsible escapist practices. Their reaction is intended specifically for those wanting to escape the morals and requirements of their own religious background, as well as those directed to a certain exclusive psychological typology. Nevertheless, Destiny is not chosen; it is, or should be, accepted religiously. Choices should not override the acceptance of one's role in space and time, nor should they override the Revelation destined for that particular time and space, which is therefore the best suited to those who are present there.

Without misunderstanding the validity of revelations previous to the Qur'an, we recognize the Qur'an as the divine revelation for us to accept: there is no turning back, because to not accept the Qur'an would be to misunderstand the validity of the message that has been offered to us. On the other hand, if all the revelations remain valid until the end of time, then the succession of such revelations is the necessary sequence of preparations and blessings divinely directed particularly toward men living in a very specific time and "jurisdiction."

Examples herein draw mostly from Buddhism or Islam not because these religions are fundamentally better than Christianity or the ancient Western religions, "Mediterranean" or not, but rather because the latter have exhausted their spiritual momentum. Christianity has suffered the most from the desecration characterizing the West today, even though it was neither a Western religion in origin nor a religion that could, in its essence or form, exhaust its spiritual vitality. I have referenced the "Eastern" religions because they are oriented toward the metaphysical perspective that is the *raison d'être* of every religion. This *raison d'être* is shared by everyone who is truly a man and who therefore wishes to completely live the ontological dimensions that belong to him, like a fish in water.

But the esoteric practices that we have mentioned and recognized are not absent from the Orthodox Church, or Eastern Christianity. They tend not only to bring fish back into the water but to make them realize that they, like all extant bodies, are made up of this water. As our Zen Master would say, "We are only an ice crystal that melts into its natural element in the heat of the sun, into its essence: water."

Another example from the Far Eastern tradition describes a drop of water. It is the substance of the ocean, but the drop will not dissolve itself into the infinite for fear of no longer feeling that it is a drop. It dreads losing its own individuality, its own limits, and its own ego. Dissolution is the "right intention." It is essential to the initiatic domain, and is the necessary perspective for the ritual to be really effective rather than leading to a "puffing up" of the "ego." This is yet another reason to adhere to a religion whose dogmas and laws place emphasis on sacrifice, rituals, and virtue, thus facilitating a willingness to experience sanctifying grace and to enter into true transcendence.

On the contrary, false masters and organizations are unfortunately nothing but a response to the needs of today's pseudo-spiritualism. These responses range from personality cults to geographic exoticism, from exclusivist elitism to sectarian fanaticism that often includes proselytizing. They include responses to the desire of some to belong to a secret society as well as the need to make changes in the world. All of these attitudes are typical of those who cannot accept, either as an historical or individual moment, their own destiny to live in their own religious community, in their own family, and in their own society.

"Praying in a taxi" also refers to maintaining the link with our centre and protecting the religious perspective even outside ritual moments. Consequently, even after leaving the Church or folding up the prayer mat, there remains a sense of dependency on Fate. We understand Fate as an expression of Divine Will, and thus the acceptance of every event of so-called "ordinary" life is a measure and method of our inner transformation. This is the only purpose of human life; we must therefore accept it as a necessary test, a sacrifice that allows us to extinguish ourselves, or, as the Sufis say, "die even before death comes." We should become like the seawater that evaporates in the heat of the sun and collects in the clouds, from which it will descend again to fertilize the land and renew the cycle of existence.

But we do not want to commit the same mistake as those who try to explain everything with rational or psychological analysis, thus ignoring the deeper motivations of processes related to essence and existence. If the affirmation, "God is here," prevails in the process related to essence, then it is impossible to ignore that, like a mask, the devil is present in the process related to existence but cannot be seen because men do not notice him or believe in him. It is said that the devil's greatest cunning is his ability to make everyone believe that he does not exist or that he is somewhere that he is not. The first idea (that the devil does not exist) typifies the contemporary attitude of people who are "logical, adult, and advanced" and beyond "medieval prejudices." The second idea of the devil massages our sectarian pride by identifying evil with our opposition and the ideas of others rather than looking for it within ourselves.

It is also said that the greatest evil is our "existence," before which all our other faults vanish.[3] Existence is "standing outside," or a lack of acceptance, or a rebellion like Lucifer's (*Iblis'*). Lucifer could not resign himself to the fact that God was and is able to bestow favors on someone else (Adam, or Man), and thus he became the eternal cause of his own damnation.[4] Rather than see evil in ourselves, we identify it in what we are not, what we do not understand, and in what others have that is different from what we have. We believe that we are the only ones who are just and right, and are thus entitled to call the others barbarians or unbelievers. We remain unaware that the devil to be fought is precisely what is within us—our ego—in our existing outside the "ocean."

This explains how the agnosticism, atheism, and materialism of the start of the century was linked to the dreams of a humanity that was supposedly better, strengthened by so-called technological progress, yet was far from God, having been replaced by the rise of the pseudo-spiritualities of today, the spread of sects and of "new religions." If the devil is inside us, we will also bring it into religion. Medieval builders spread monsters and goblins throughout the nooks and crannies of cathedrals, thereby detracting from their value as houses of God. We today erect cathedrals to evil: with our reforms, our protests against the dogmas and revealed laws, our schisms from traditional organizations, or worse yet, with our dissident sects opposed to constitutional authority, we create houses of the devil. So we dedicate ourselves to alleged reconstructions of dead traditions or purely exterior renovations of those still alive; we want to build a paradise on Earth rather than try to improve ourselves. We forget that the true Kingdom is not of this world and that, in order to enter

---

3. The great master of Sufism, Junayd al-Baghdadi (d. 298/910), said, "Nothing benefitted me more than the benefit I derived from some poetry that I heard [being sung by a slave girl, among which is the hemistich:] 'Your existence is a sin to which no other sin compares'" Ibn 'Imad (d. 1089/1679), *Shadharat al-dhahab* (Beirut: Dar Ihya' al-Turath al-'Arabi, n.d.), v. 2, p. 229. Also noted by Al-Khatib al-Baghdadi, Ibn Khallikan, Ibn Kathir, and al-Safidi in their histories.

4. See Qur'an 2:30-34, 38:71-78.

Heaven, we must become like innocent children.[5]

When my son Yahya was learning to pray, he made strange plays on words with his elementary Arabic. Sometimes he confused Arabic with English, the language that my wife and I used to understand each other because neither of us knew the mother tongue of the other. All this seems very complicated, as always happens when it is a question of "me" and "you," "my" and "your." A proverb says, "Happy is the man who never says 'I.'" In fact, when some of the ancient Arab sages had to talk about themselves, they used the pronoun *nahnu*, or "we," because they believed that only Allah, God, can say *ana*: I. It would be so simple and clear if Man could only speak in His name, certainly not on behalf of himself, but in the name of God, in the name of Allah. The Arabic expression *bismiLlah*, "in the name of God," consecrates all acts of every true believer.

Allah means "God" and stems from the contraction of the Arabic definite article *al*, the equivalent of the English word "the," with the word *ilah*, or "god." The word Allah renders the idea of being absolute, in the sense of "The God," God, the Divinity, the one God. This not only indicates that there is only one God and not many gods, but above all, this means that God is One; He is all that there is; there is nothing and no one else outside Him; there is no other God but God Himself. This final statement makes up the first part of the testimony of Islamic faith: *la ilaha illa Allah*. Coupled with the affirmation that Muhammad is the Prophet of Allah (*Muhammad rasul Allah*), this phrase makes every man or woman that recites it at any moment of his or her life a *Muslim*. The testimony is the first of the five pillars upon which Islamic Law, or *shari'ah*, is built. The other four are: prayer (*salat*), fasting (*sawm*), almsgiving (*zakat*), and pilgrimage (*hajj*).

To return to my son Yahya, who had inherited his father's bad habit of not pronouncing "*h*"s, he found that the words *Islam* or *Muslim* contained the same consonants as the word *(bi)Ismi-Llah*, and that a *Muslim* is a man who lives *bismi-Llah*, that is, in the name of God. Indeed, in the name of whom else could he live if there is no other, if there is no one else except "Him," no one else except God himself, who is his only God, our only God, the God of all men? No one but

---

5. Matthew 18:3. Al-Bukhari reports a hadith in which the Prophet says: "I looked at Paradise and found poor people forming the majority of its inhabitants," (*Sahih Bukhari*, book 4, volume 54, hadith 464)

He who is really his true Self, our true Self, the Self of us all?

One day at the seashore, Yahya told me, "If only Allah is, then we only exist as a reflection of His Being."

I answered him that the word "reflection" was well chosen, since there is only one sun but millions of lights reflect on the sea. Likewise, there is only one sea, but it produces many waves and foam that would not exist without water. If he looked at the sea he would not see the waves and foam, and if he concentrated on the water's reflections, he would not see the Sun despite knowing that the Sun creates them. "It is necessary," I added, "that we, in forming the waves of life, remain in the sea and follow the tides, that we accept our fate as the will of God, and that we obey His Law instead of separating from the ocean to form a dead puddle where we would do nothing other than exist."

"It would be better then," replied Yahya, "to make a mistake in the name of God than to do something in our own name."

I told him that he could never do harm if he truly acted in the name of God. Allah would guide him because "the movement of the key is guided by the movement of the hand, and both are movements of the hand of the Lord."

"Do you remember, Yahya," I continued, "what your mother told us when she was learning the art of archery in her native Japan? She told us that when she really learned to shoot, she could do it even with her eyes closed or blindfolded or in the dark, and she managed to hit the target all the same. And she said, in such a way that we thought she had made a grammatical error and the sentence was referring to the bow: 'I was not shooting, He did it.'"

"Do not forget," I added, "that the name of Allah has an "*h*" at the end, and we can also refer to Allah just with this "*h*," the pronoun *Hu*, a contraction of *Huwa* that means He or Him. This word expresses the spirit of His Name in its sound and His perennial breathing in us which makes our heart beat, as if we ourselves are always repeating His name."

"I understand," Yahya said, "what Mother wanted to say when she exclaimed, 'He did it.' She meant, 'He did it,' that is, He, God, or better, *Huwa*." And Yahya cried with joy, repeating and repeating, "*Huwa, Hu, Hu, Hu*."

Assisi 1986. Shaykh Abd al-Wahid Pallavicini
and Pope John Paul II.

Of the Beginning and of the End[1]

"I was a hidden treasure"—God says in a holy tradition revealed to the Prophet Muhammad—"and I wanted to be known, so I created the world."[2] Thus the very reason for the creation of the world is God's desire to be known by Man who "dies unto himself, before dying."[3] In the words of the Prophet, to achieve this state we must "worship God as if we saw Him because, although we do not see Him, He sees us."[4]

This is the essence of primordial Tradition (*din al-qayyimah*). It is the foundation of the purest Islamic orthodoxy, and of the unity that transcends the numerous Revelations. It is the Truth that was never revealed because it is identified with God Himself, who is neither Jewish, nor Christian, nor Muslim.

While we respect the providential differences between the Traditions, we must emphasize their shared essential identity. This identity is a truth that, in varying degrees, remains conscious for the entire cycle of humanity's existence. According to all of the sacred doctrines, at the beginning of the cycle there is only one Tradition to which there corresponds a single human "model." In Islam, this model takes the name *al-insan al-kamil* (Universal Man). The gradual departure from God, or Man's "fall" from this primordial state, made necessary the subsequent Revelations (which, because of their differences in form and together with the "fall" itself, once again veil the one Tradition, the only Reality).

---

1. Translation of the eponymous article and other chapters from the same book: *Islam interiore, la ricerca della verità nella religione islamica*, Il Saggiatore, Milan, 2002.

2. Ibn 'Arabi mentions this holy tradition (*hadith qudsi, or God's words repeated by the Prophet*) in a number of instances in his *al-Futuhat al-Makkiya* (Beirut: Dar Sadir, n.d.), e.g., vol. 2, p. 112, question #116, What is the wine of love? (*ma sharab al-hubb*)

3. Tirmidhi transmitted the hadith, "Be in the world like a stranger or traveller and count yourself to be among the folk of the graves." Ibn Majah transmitted the hadith, "Repent (*tubu*) before you die!" A saying sometimes regarded as a hadith is, "Die before you die!"

4. Both Bukhari and Muslim included in their "authentic" (*sahih*) collections the hadith in which the Prophet, in defining "*ihsan*," stated, "[It is] that you worship God as if you see God; and if you do not see God, [realize] that He sees you."

The subsequent revelation served to renew remembrance of the divine origin of the Creation.

These aspects of doctrine are crucial to understanding religion in general and Islam in particular. Though the Revelation of the Qur'an took place in the seventh century AD, the Islamic tradition began with Adam, the first man and first Prophet of Islam. The tradition then proceeded through Muhammad, Seal of the Prophets, with whom the cycle of Revelation ends. Thus Islam unites the legacy of all the previous Prophets into a synthesis that has its own eschatological *raison d'être*. It must be the ark that will enable the transition from this cycle to the next. In fact, the eschatological moment will see Christ return again in the Second Coming, not to bring a new Revelation, but because he is the Seal of Sanctity and Judgment who is called to verify that the hearts of men are truly turned toward the divine Unity.[5]

However, there is no reason to fear that the cycle foreseen (since the beginning of creation) by all of the theocentric and theocratic sacred books of true traditional civilizations might close at any given moment of history. Nor is there a reason to fool ourselves into believing in an indefinite linear progression and a supposed continuing evolution of humanity.

The work of René Guénon must be understood according to this eschatological perspective regarding the end of the present cycle and the preparation for the next. But today are we truly aware of the fact that, since his death, the end of this cycle has drawn much nearer to us? Are we really aware that the dissolving influences that characterize our current cycle have penetrated ever more deeply, even into traditional forms?

In fact, these are no longer the times that René Guénon called "solidification of the world," when it was still possible to distinguish between religious faith and atheistic materialism. In the present "dissolution," which became dominated by psychic forces and the complete loss of any traditional reference, even rational ones, once upward access was closed to most people, even the "elect" are deceived by the appearance of an inverted spirituality which is

---

5. Both Bukhari and Muslim transmit hadiths confirming the second coming of Jesus. Ibn 'Arabi refers to Jesus ('Isa) as the "seal of sanctity" (*khatm al-wilaya*) *Futuhat al-Makkiya* [Beirut: Dar Sadir, n.d.], v. 2, p. 49, question #13 "Who is the one who is worthy of being the seal of the saints, just as the Muhammad (peace and blessings be upon him) is worthy of being the seal of the prophets?"

only a parody of the true and the sacred, as it appears for instance in the growing market of new "religions."

Of course, decadence has existed since the world began: it existed when Adam was expelled from the Garden of Eden. But never before, in any part of the world other than in the West, has there been such an inversion of values. The proponents of secularism as a false spirituality demand that institutional hierarchies, the purpose of human life, and metaphysical principles themselves should all be independent of the Creator. They set themselves up as the only judges on earth, all in the name of freedom of choice and equality among all beings, and yet they reject the nature of Man as the only creature made in the image and likeness of God. Numerous circumstances in the West have created fertile ground for the growth of religions lacking inner dimension, the development of hierarchies that have lost their exemplary character, and the birth of men without the need for ritual practice. This has occurred because everything that was sacred or spiritual has been reduced to a psychological and human level. Hence many people no longer believe in the effectiveness of Grace. They believe only in the philanthropic expressions of those who have forgotten that "if God was made Man (in Christianity) then it was only in order for Man to become God" [6] and not in order for humanity to be worshipped as an idol.

Once again, the typical modern trend toward globalism, generality, and uniformity—caused by the misconception that Man is simply a number in a collective mass—becomes evident. It is no longer possible to distinguish between those who try to realize Man's resemblance to the Divine and those who avoid it and hurtle themselves into a spiritual conundrum that is entirely earthly. These unfortunates refuse the help of others who have received a specific sacred function, preferring to fight for "human rights" rather than fulfill divine duties.

It is said that the East does not understand the West but rather accepts it, both by recognizing it as the complement to the Pole that belongs to God alone, and by allowing itself to be corrupted by the desecration that comes from it. Meanwhile, the West understands the East as posing a danger to its survival and therefore does not accept it. This danger is not posed by the various forms

---

6. Originally stated by Athanasius (*De inc.* 54, 3: PG 25, 192B), this is an official aspect of church doctrine. (*Catechism of the Catholic Church*, 2nd edition).

of secularization that correspond to the desecration coming from the West but rather by the spirituality that has always come from the East—*ex Oriente Lux*. The West first tried to counter this spirituality during the time of the spread of Christianity nearly two thousand years ago.

We do not desire to force the world to faith nor do we want to convert all men to Islam. The Qur'anic expression, "Religion—to God—is Islam" (*inna ad-dina 'inda Allahi al-Islam*),[7] is correctly understood by translating the word *Islam* as "submission to God." We want to consider Islam not only as the last call to the unicity of God—"I bear witness that there is no god except God" (*ashhadu an la ilaha illa Allah*)—but also as a call to submission to His Will and His laws that were given by the One God to all the peoples of the world in different eras through the teachings of those prophets whom He sent since the time of the first man and the first Islamic prophet, Adam.

> If God had wanted, He would have made of you one community, but this He did not do, in order to test you in what was given to you. Compete, therefore, with good works, which all return to God, and then He will inform you about those things about which you are now in disagreement.[8]

This is not our attempt to again preach a doctrine that, in the course of fourteen centuries, has providentially spread to a specific geographical area with over one billion believers. Without having actually spread throughout the entire world, Islam is nonetheless universal because God made its message for all men on earth. Its relatively small European following (in comparison to its followings on other continents) is not only due to a Western lack of knowledge of its principles or to the opposition of other Western religious institutions. It is due above all to the spiritual aridity of modern Westerners and their hostility toward Eastern spirituality and the sacred dimension of divine Revelation, both of which were originally present in the Revelations. These too were Eastern and were oriented toward the metaphysical fulfillment, or reunion with God, to which they traced their origin.

It is not appropriate for a European, or anyone for that matter, to pronounce the *shahadah* (the testimony of Islamic faith) to

---

7. Qur'an 3:19.
8. Qur'an 5:48.

another person if he has not yet found faith in God. The path of submission consists, first of all, of *iman* (faith). Then, *insha'Allah* (God willing), one achieves *islam* (submission to God). The path finally leads to *ihsan* (spiritual perfection). Therefore, conversion to Islam cannot take place without prior conversion to God, just as one may not proclaim "*la ilaha illa al-Islam*" ("There is no divinity but Islam") in the place of saying *la ilaha illa Allah*. Although some exceptional Europeans have spoken about the transcendent unity of the Revelations as well as the uniqueness of God, those who are approaching Islam today must still have a sense of the immanence of God and of His spiritual presence both in this world and within themselves.

Churches today host little talk about God and only preach about peace, while in mosques there is an overabundance of talk about war. Muslims seem to betray their own testimony of faith – "there is no god but God" – by making an idol of their own religion, as if to say that there is no god, or truth, except in Islam. Christianity also emphasizes hegemonic exclusivity by reinforcing the concept *Extra Ecclesiam nulla salus* ("Outside the Church there is no salvation").[9] The insistence that European roots lie only in Christian tradition still endures. This claim makes the Christian "unconvertible" not because Europeans are blind to the "unity of traditions," but because they are still tied to a mentality that is at the root of every deviation from present-day Catholicism and is continually reinforced by the West of today. The "unconvertible" Westerners are those who do not want to, or are actually unable to, reorient: not only toward original orthodoxy but even less toward the metaphysics of the primordial Tradition that God has provided once more in His last Revelation, Islam.

On the one hand, neither aversion to the decadence of one's Tradition of origin nor the hope of being able to follow an initiatory path can justify conversion to a religion, even if it is subsequent and does not involve any apostasy. On the other hand, authentic conversion requires both attraction and sincere adherence to the doctrine expressed by a new Revelation.

Can strongly reaffirming the uniqueness of God (*tawhid*) and the reality of *al-insan al-kamil* (universal man) induce the rediscovery of an orthodoxy forgotten in the historical and theologi-

---

9. *Catechism of the Catholic Church*, #845-46 and ascribed to Cyprian (d. 258).

cal vicissitudes of an institution like the Catholic Church? Can it reintroduce the possibility of a truly metaphysical understanding within a path that has not been influenced, in recent times, by the need for hierarchical dependence at an exoteric level?

If the word "universal" (in the expression "universal man") connotes our desire to proceed toward the One, then the difficulties faced by Catholics in conceiving of a return to the original Principle perhaps stem from Catholicism's dualistic tendencies— be they disguised as "Christic mysteries," poor interpretations of the "mystery of the dual Nature of Christ," or as a mystical attitude toward "love for each other."

Despite the Promethean ideas of some modern Europeans who would like to grasp the secret by following their own will power, in fact the Principle can only be truly realized through the transparency of someone who has been able "to die before dying."[10] These are the words of the Prophet, who, even at the time of his death, retired to Medina in order to preserve for Mecca its absoluteness as symbol of the Universal Temple.

As for the theme of the Apocalypse, I wish to emphasize that there is no difference between eschatologies according to the Jewish, Christian, or Islamic doctrines. Nor is there a religious evolutionism because, in the temporal succession of Revelations, God does not assign "one" to Jews, "two" to Christians, or "three" to Muslims. There is only one single eschatological destiny for humanity, the world, and each one of us.

I wish to clarify, however, the fact that Judaism makes no mention of the eschatological figure of the Antichrist. In addition, the traditional information of Christianity itself presents the second coming of Christ in a much more indeterminate way than the doctrine found in the ultimate Revelation of the cycle, Islam. However, these previous forms can benefit from certain tools for understanding offered by the successive Revelations, particularly in the Abrahamic traditions and especially regarding eschatology. For example, Christianity could benefit from the following conceptual tool of Islam: All Muslims believe in Jesus as the "Spirit of God" (*Ruh Allah*) and await his second coming. Hence, Christians could enhance their understanding of the second coming (with important implications for their understanding of the Antichrist) if they were to keep this conception of Jesus as the "Spirit of God"

---

10. A hadith ascribed to the Prophet is "Die before you die" (discussed above).

in mind. They must recognize that the Jesus of Islam is not de-rived from Christianity, as Christians might think. On the contrary, Islam teaches that Christianity originated in Christ just as Christ comes from God, and just as the Word of God, manifest in the Holy Qur'an, contains Jesus and describes his Presence.

Keeping this Islamic conceptual tool in mind would then en-able Christians (and anyone interested in Christ) to ask the ques-tion: "Could this God's Spirit (as it is expressed in Islam) have been providential at a certain moment for a certain purpose?" Con-sequently, such a question would then serve as a stepping-stone to an answer such as, "The possible precursors necessitating this Qur'anic clarification may have been both the degeneration of the *Corpus Christi* as an ecclesiastical institution as well as the hu-manization of the spiritual figure of Jesus that caused believers to forget his divine Nature. This could have "led astray even the elect, if that were possible,"[11] according to the Gospel expression referring to the one who surely lacks divine nature and who would manifest himself before Christ would.

It is important to distinguish between Christ and Christianity precisely because there is a very real danger today that Christians will confuse or are confusing the defense of the *Corpus Christi* with the propagation of the decadent ideas of a West to which they also consider themselves faithful. The danger, of course, is confus-ing the Antichrist with Christ. The Antichrist, which has no divine nature, will presume to impersonate the figure of a Christ; in con-tradiction of the Trinitarian dogma of Christian doctrine, he will proclaim himself not just god, but "the God" of Christianity.

The Antichrist will also present himself in such a form that all those who have not remained faithful to the Truth—no matter which religion they belong to—will mistake him for the one who, in their original doctrine, should be their spiritual Pole (*qutb*) *par excellence* at the end of time. Thus the Jews will confuse him with the Messiah, while Christians and Muslims will confuse him with Christ at the second coming. Muslims who are also awaiting the coming of the Mahdi (the well-guided *imam* who should precede and prepare us for the second coming of Jesus) are vulnerable to falling into error by confusing the Antichrist with the Mahdi and the Mahdi with Christ himself.

Some people have wanted to identify the Antichrist with vari-

11. Matthew XXIV, 24.

ous obscure figures of the past. Others have wanted to identify the Antichrist with defeated materialistic ideologies. Still others consider the Antichrist to be something left over from the imagination of our ancestors. In the light of the teachings of René Guénon, however, the Antichrist will present an anticipatory parody of both what should be the final eschatological reconstitution of the two powers (spiritual authority and temporal power) as well as the momentary illusion of the restoration of world peace, the harbinger of the end.

Now it is two thousand years after the birth of Sayiduna 'Isa, Jesus. As we await his return at the end of time, it is important to remember that, beyond the eschatology that is common to all the true Revelations, our personal eschatologies also exist. In the Holy Qur'an God says: "Soon will We show them our Signs in the (furthest) regions (of the earth) and in their own souls, until it becomes manifest to them that this is the Truth"[12] As men and women born in the Western space–time continuum marked by the first coming of Jesus, it is our responsibility to know how to wait for the *parousia*, the true Second Coming. This event alone will finally reconcile us to God through a re-opened Golden Door in Jerusalem.[13] This will be the true ecumenism at the summit, and the only ecumenism able to move toward a real peace. This true peace comes not only from justice and is not obtainable at any price— it will be based on a higher justice that can only come from the mutual recognition of the spiritual validity of our different faiths within the Abrahamic tradition to which we all belong. What can really bring together sincere believers is the sense of "sacrifice" in the original and etymological meaning of the word, that of *sacrum facere*: to make every moment of our lives sacred, by means of the religious forms that God has given to each of us.

In these very special times that seem to "undermine" even religions, we have a responsibility to intervene and learn how to make good this "crisis" that touches us all. We mean "crisis" in the etymological sense of the term that refers to "judgment," or the moment of truth contained within the revelation of the true nature

---

12. Qur'an 41:53.

13. Walled up during Ottoman times, the Golden Door or *Bab al-rahmah*, is in the Eastern Wall of the Masjid al-Aqsa in Jerusalem. (In the eastern wall of the Haram al-Sharif, up from the garden of Gethsemane, opening onto the Dome of the Rock.) A Christian belief predicts that Jesus will open it during his second coming.

of things. For us as men of faith, evil dwells only in the deception that wants to make us look elsewhere and forget God. On the other hand, our familiar eschatology does not describe "the end of the world" but, in the words of Shaykh 'Abd al-Wahid Yahya Guénon, only "the end of *a* world."

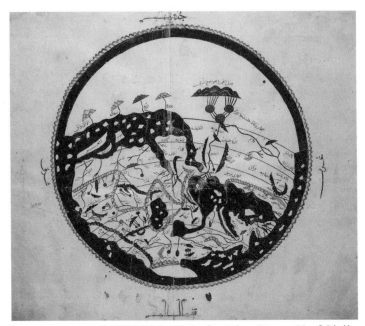

The world map of Al-Idrisi in 1154 for King Roger II of Sicily.
The map had south at its top.

Across the World's Center[1]

In 1995, the year that my book *Inner Islam*[2] was published in French, Bruno Hapel asked several times in an article[3]: Where are the "faithful servants" of René Guénon? Why are they not trying to be servants? And why do they refuse to be guided by him? Or, even worse, why do they let themselves be fooled by "those who present themselves as faithful interpreters" but "act as screens that mask and distort the work that they should be representing?" Since then, things have not changed at all. If anything, they have gotten worse. Bruno Hapel's attempt to resurrect several texts by René Guénon, in order to return to Hindu doctrine and the teachings of Ramana Maharshi by grafting them at least in part to Christian religious practice, seems to have been short-lived.

This lack of discrimination precisely illustrates the way of thinking typical of the West today. Believing it is able to survive by "standing on the ruins," ultimately this thinking only brings about its own ruin instead of truly trying to know itself. If the "Truth defends itself without help," then the discernment necessary to understanding the difference between the Truth and its counterfeits becomes of increasingly vital importance. There is a difference between the devil and his mask just as there is a difference between earth (which is, in the words of Evola, "telluric, Demeterian, feminine, and chthonic") and heaven, which Guénon described as between the manifest and the unmanifest.[4] We could add the following descriptions: between the mental and spiritual, between *asura*s and *deva*s, and between demons and angels;[5] as well as between the symbol and symbolized, and between traditionalism and Tradition, or in other words, between anti-tradition and every true revealed tradition. These concepts are certainly relative, but only compared with an Absolute. They are

---

1. Text partly drawn from *Islam interiore* (Milan: Il Saggiatore, 2002), with a final comment about the meaning of the presence of Islam in Europe, from Yahya Pallavicini, *L'Islam in Europa* (Il Saggiatore, Milan, 2004).

2. Abd al-Wahid Pallavicini, *L'islam intérieur: la spiritualité universelle dans la religion islamique* (Paris : Bartillat, 1995).

3. Bruno Hapel "Actions et réactions concordantes," *Vers la Tradition* 59:35.

4. See René Guénon, *La Grande Triade* (Paris: Gallimard, 1957).

5. For Guénon on *asura*s and *deva*s, see Guénon, *Symbolism of the Cross,* ibid., p. 111.

57

not "individual" and are not "phenomenological"; they are Real. In short, this is the difference between physics and metaphysics. It is not at all the "metaphysics of sex"[6] but rather that of the Spirit.

Integrity, therefore, is not ideological, because ideology breaks while trying to cleave the rock of reality. Integrity is instead spiritual, because spiritual truth knows how to bend like bamboo when the wind blows. Integrity knows the true nature of the world and the nature of Man's inward and outward aspects. It is exemplified by the kind of behavior that is turned toward the East and that caused the Muslim saint Rabia al-Adawiyya to say, "I am a hypocrite as long as I feed off of this world but live for the other."[7]

Therefore it is hardly surprising that just as a Muslim "disciple" of René Guénon was unable to go beyond the limits of cosmology, some Christians, though well-informed about the work of Shaykh 'Abd al-Wahid Yahya Guénon, have encountered "a theological and ecclesiological impossibility in simultaneously being both Christian and followers of Guénon." As a matter of fact, the theological emphasis put by Christian churches, including the Roman Catholic Church, on the fact that they are the only religion to own the "means of salvation," acts as a barrier to acknowledge the action of divine Providence— or of the primordial Tradition—through, and within other religions. Paradoxically, other Christians have come to reject both Christianity and "the universalism of René Guénon." They chose to become Muslims not because of the Truth of Islam, or Guénon's teachings about the primordial Tradition, but because they considered that they had no more choice for their religious lives, as far as they saw Islam as the only traditional orthodox form after "the theological innovation of 809 CE," that is, the time when the Holy Ghost was understood by the Catholic Church as also proceeding "from the Son" and not only "from the Father" (the well-known issue called *Filioque* in Christian theology). This standpoint may call for three comments. First, to our eyes, the only good reason that should lead us to embrace a religion is because we believe it is *true*. It does not mean only the kind of intellectual acknowledgement to which the doctrine of the primordial Tradition leads us; it means that we recognize, and answer God's call to us *through this religion*. Second, we must also acknowledge that

---

6. See Julius Evola, *La Metafisica del sesso*. (Edizioni Mediterranee, Roma, 1996).

7. For Rabi'a, see Farid al-Din Attar, Rabi'a al-Adawiya, from *Muslim Saints and Mystics*, trans. A.J. Arberry (London:Routledge & Kegan Paul, 1983).

the doctrine of the Spirit in the Catholic Church has been becoming always more "specific," to say the least. A little bit later, after the 8th ecumenical Council of 869 CE, the Catholic Church began to teach the unity of the human soul. It did not distinguish any more between the Spirit and the soul.[8] These facts contributed to flatten the view of the Human being and of his path to God, and deepened the gap between Roman Catholicism on the one hand, and Eastern Christianity, Judaism, and Islam on the other. Third, at the end, we should all be deeply convinced that it is not the content of our minds, nor theological concepts, that save us, but God, the Unique, who acts in us provided we sincerely turns ourselves towards Him.

The Western Islamic context seems to have experienced equal difficulty, even without considering the Swiss and American vicissitudes or the Italian ones, be they Masonic or relating to Julius Evola. In France, Michel Vâlsan, who unfortunately is no longer here to confirm this, told me that he found it difficult to make his disciples understand Islam. He expressed concern that once he passed away they would be able to refer only to his personality. Even among those who describe themselves as "disciples" of René Guénon, there are some who believed that they should distance themselves from his orthodox teaching in favor of syncretism with other religions or with other organizations. Yet clearly one cannot regain the "Lost Word" solely through texts and documents. There must be a direct personal transmission of a spiritual influence through an initiatic chain consisting of a continuous succession of Masters and organizations that date back as far as the prophetic Revelation.

René Guénon had tried in vain to fight the mistakes and excuses that deceived generations of his alleged followers who erroneously believed they were referring to his teachings or those of his so-called successors. In light of the events that concern them, we assert that these errors are merely the result of deviant ideas that go back to that period.

Guénon always expressly stated that he never had disciples, since he did not consider himself a spiritual Master or a *guru*. He instead acted as a *pandit*, or someone who was merely passing on the doctrine to people without acting as a spiritual guide. He himself remained connected to an Egyptian branch of an Islamic brotherhood called the Shadhiliyah.

Contrary to what Bruno Hapel would have preferred for West-

---

8. The Council of Aix-la-Chapelle was held in the ninth century. It was a prelude to the schism between the Catholic and Orthodox Church.

erners (he thought they should "become the real custodians of their tradition"), the Islamic tradition teaches that when the Sun rises from the West only the Westerners themselves will remain faithful to the Truth. A community of forty men will be formed to guard the Tradition, namely the Primordial Tradition that René Guénon described to us. Perhaps this community could only start to form exactly forty years from the day he left us.

Besides Guénon, the other major influence on this nascent community was Shaykh Ahmad ibn Idris. Unlike other spiritual Masters of that era, Shaykh Ahmad ibn Idris was not a founding Shaykh of a *tariqah* in the strict sense of the word; he was the interpreter of the essence of Sufism, known as the Muhammadan pathway (*al-tariqah al-muhammadiyah*). The life of Shaykh Ahmad ibn Idris (1760-1837) is summed up by his patient adherence to this path of righteousness—the shortest path to God. He was certainly reconnected to the *turuq* (paths), particularly the Shadhiliyah, through his spiritual Masters, but he is recognized primarily as one who passed on the blessing of the initiatic chain of the Khadiriyah, named after Al-Khidr, this mysterious prophet that holy men sometimes encounter in their spiritual path.

Shaykh Ahmad ibn Idris has said:

> We take no pride in any creature whatever creature he is; we place no hope in any creature for anything whatsoever. We are slaves of God, journeying towards God, fearing nothing save God, hoping for nothing save God, clinging to nothing save God, and placing trust in nothing save God. Whoever clings only to God is guided to the straight path, and whoever places his trust in God is requited, as in the statement of our Prophet and Master Muhammad, the Messenger of God: "That which a human being fears has mastery over him, but if a human being fears nothing save God, nothing other than God will have mastery over him." And the Prophet also said: "A human being is dependent upon that which leads him to that to which he aspires, but if a human being aspires to nothing other than God, God will lead him to nothing else."[9]

Shaykh Ahmad ibn Idris' teachings call for all aspects of life to be-

---

9. R. S. O'Fahey, *The Enigmatic Saint: Ahmad ibn Idris and the Idrisi Tradition* (Chicago: Northwestern University Press, 1990), pp. 79-80.

come sacred, even outside ritual times and at every moment. According to the perpetual prayer of the hesychast remembrance of God, we must focus on the sacred "with every glance and with every breath," so that, once we have left the retreat or folded the prayer rug, there is no return to an individualistic view of things. Such continual remembrance causes every act and every thought of ordinary life to remain turned in the direction of prayer, even though Mecca is no longer faced ritually or literally but ontologically.

The Shaykh's life was so simple and upright that we know very few of its details. He bore witness with great spiritual transparency in the service of God. The greatness of this "Enigmatic Saint" is evidenced by the deep and lasting mark he left on his followers and their subsequent generations. His spiritual influence shines forth to the four cardinal points of the Islamic world. It may be surprising to Westerners that a religion like Islam, which has neither clergy nor monasticism, nevertheless requires a strict form of transmission when it comes to its inner or esoteric dimension. This transmission is achieved through a clear hierarchy and the establishment of initiatic organizations: the Islamic brotherhoods, or *turuq*, meaning "pathways."

The most important elements are the following: to receive the blessedness or spiritual influence (*barakah*) that dates back to the founder of the brotherhood; to follow the method; and to have the right intention when participating in the rite. Possessing right intention is a natural state for every religious person but is rather difficult for anyone who approaches this practice without the true theocentric perspective that only the Master who personally knows the candidate can direct and eventually awaken. Moreover, the Master, the brotherhood, and the practice of the method are merely instruments for spiritual achievement and the expression of a true vocation. Vocation thus manifests itself in a right intention to overcome one's own individuality. This is certainly not achieved through the self-satisfaction of belonging to an élite group, the purely outward search for a secret organization, or by seeking a Master whom one wishes to revere as the spiritual pole of the present age. Instead of assisting devotees in overcoming their individuality, such a master becomes the center of a personality cult.

We must overcome the self in order to eliminate the atavistic splitting or doubling that makes us spectators of our own experiences. As long as we remain spectators, it is almost as if we have performed certain rites to see what effect they had on us, and not for the effect itself. The effect cannot occur so long as we have not re-established our identity with our being and its integrity, or so long as we remain distant observers of our ritual participation. Of course, the rite in itself does not suffice without actively engaging knowledge of the symbol and without the right intention to participate in sacredness. If Knowledge without practice is sterile, then practice without Knowledge is the same.

"The traditional way is sincerity," wrote Shaykh at-Tadili (d. 1229-30 CE). In other words, true esotericism must assume not only (1) the initiatic chain, which passes on a spiritual influence through the regular succession of the Masters; (2) the spiritual community to rely upon at every occasion; and most importantly, (3) the method of the invocation of the Name of God (*dhikr*); but it must also (4) require the intention of the believers to be deeply and completely sincere by consistently following orthodox belief with orthodox practice.

Some obstacles that we must overcome during our journey on the path of spiritual realization are not obstacles of real difficulty but rather imaginary problems. Their origins are of an emotional nature common to the Western mentality. The literature that we will call "romantic," produced by Eastern authors for the use of Western readers, describes these emotions.

A classic example of such "complexes" (to use the abhorrent psychoanalytical term that does, however, denote an effective inhibition) is considering oneself unworthy of such an undertaking. These thoughts misunderstand one's ontological nature: in fact, every person is a candidate for spiritual enlightenment, and his or her life is precisely the sole test that must be faced to achieve this goal. We attribute the reason for this "complex" to the damage on the human psyche caused by psychoanalysis. Since psychoanalysis today ignores the Divine Being and minimizes the existence of the devil, one forgets the mercy of God—who "takes ninety-nine steps towards he who takes only one towards Him"— as well as the fact that we are not responsible for the evil suggestions that come to us, but perhaps only for listening to them.

One day Husayn ibn Mansur al-Hallaj (857–922 CE) was asked what he thought about esoteric teaching (*madhhab al-batin*). "About which do you wish me to speak, the false or true esotericism (*batin al-batil aw batin al-Haqq*)? As for true esotericism, its exoteric aspect is *shari'ah* (Islamic law); and whoever truly follows the exoteric aspect of the *shari'ah* will discover its esoteric aspect, which is none other than the knowledge of God (*ma'rifah bi'llah*). As for false esotericism, its esoteric and exoteric aspects are equally horrible and disgusting. Therefore do not become involved in it."[10]

Each claim to an inner aspect detached from this living source (which is the Knowledge of Allah discovered by following true esotericism together with the exoteric way) indeed constitutes a dive into the stagnant waters of the psychic world. These corners and labyrinths of the psyche, although not "grossly" visible, do not escape the dominion of form. The psychic, in fact, still belongs to the "outward," whereas only the spiritual can legitimately be called "inner."

True spirituality is the Spirit's work within us. To speak in somewhat theological terms, it means waiting for Grace. This is easily understood from a metaphysical point of view, since no action in an "inferior" world (such as the formal world of which we are directly conscious) can affect the *super-formal* states of the "superior" worlds. At the same time, however, the spiritual path is the opposite of quietism. We must prepare ourselves for Grace is by using the available material means that God has placed near us. These means are the first manifestation of divine Grace. There also exist certain trends that lead non-Muslim believers to practice Islamic initiatic rituals. Sometimes these participants anticipate possible conversion to Islam, a religion that is still largely unknown to them and certainly less practiced. Those who conceived of this deviatory practice derived it from a misunderstanding of Shaykh al-Alawi's teachings. Shaykh al-Alawi is said to have brought Sufism to the West and Guénon himself sent some of his correspondents to study under him. Yet some writers claimed that the Shaykh, "a Muslim Saint of the Twentieth Century," had come "for everybody" and not just for Muslims. Another idea that spread among traditionalist circles asserted that Christians, by the mere fact of their position, were all virtual initiates and could therefore turn to a Master "no matter the religion of the latter."

---

10. Ibn al-Sa'i, *Kitab Akhbar al-Hallaj,* ed. and trans. by Louis Massignon and Paul Kraus, p. 19 (Arabic), p. 61 (French).

These abhorrent trends spurred the creation of Western organizations that are nothing more than a parody of the traditional *turuq*. They also engendered today's swarm of pseudo-teachers who do not demand strict adherence to the religious law of the Tradition to which they presume to belong. Consequently, such teachers cannot pass on any effective influence or valid spiritual instruction leading to possible spiritual enlightenment. Their guidance is like the imaginary fruit of a tree that has had its roots cut.

Appropriate criticism of the mystification of the sacred does not constitute an excuse for those who do not want to fit into traditional structures. We know that error and corruption exist outside those institutions as well as within the heart of them. Yet there are not only bad Masters: there are also bad disciples. Principles should not be confused with organizations, nor rites with the men who administer them.

Herein lies the difficulty: the attraction to the inner dimension was linked mainly to Westerners' loss of the sense of God's immanence, specifically the loss of God's presence in the world and within themselves. Because of this experience, many Westerners have merely developed a "conceptualization" of God. The words of Shaykh 'Abd al-Wahid Yahya Guénon best describe this connection: "When authentic representatives of a Tradition reach the point where their way of thinking does not differ very greatly from that of its opponents, you may ask how much life this Tradition still has in its present condition."[11]

It is, nevertheless, necessary to push onwards as a witness, sometimes leaving only a message "in the ether" to be collected by a blessed community of men and women in the years to follow.

> The increasingly conspicuous presence of Muslims in the West, also of European origin, acquires a special significance: perhaps it is in this sense that the prophetic words, "Islam is foreign born and will end foreign," can be interpreted;[12] or again, as the traditional saying announces, as one of the signs of the end of time, the fact that "the Sun will set in the East and rise in the West."[13] With this, we do not want to say

---

11. Guénon, *Initiation et Realisation Spirituelle,* ibid;

12. *Bada'a al-islam ghariban wa-sa-ya'udu ka-ma bada'a ghariban, Sahih Muslim, Kitab al-Iman*, on the authority of Abu Hurayra.

13. Cf., *Qala rasul Allah: La taqumu al-sa'ah hatta tatlu'a al-shamsu min maghribiha:* "On the authority of Abu Hurayra, the Messenger of God said, 'The

or hope, as others do, for the mass conversion of Westerners to Islam. Nor do we especially want to exclude the presence of well-oriented people in other religious confessions of the West. We only want to consider the importance of certain spiritual presences and the part that Western Muslims might have in bearing witness to their own traditional reorientation. It is significant that in this process of balance between the Islamic world and the contemporary West, the European Islamic community is called upon to play a role, not only as a bridge between East and West, but also as a model of integrity and religious universality that is truly lived.[14]

[Last] hour will not be established until the sun rises in the west.'" *Sahih Bukhari,* ibid., *Kitab al-Tafsir, al-'Araf, bab "la yanfa'u nafsan imanuha,"* vol. 4, p. 1697, #4359-60.

14. Yahya Pallavicini, "Oriente e Occidente" in *Islam in Europa: Riflessioni di un imam italiano* (Milano: Il Saggiatore, 2004), p. 140.

A traditional islamic wedding in the Al-Wahid Mosque
of Milan in 2005.

The *ahmadi idrisi shadhuli* brethren with Shaykh Abd-al-Wahid
in a meeting in the French Alps in the village of Les Orres,
in a place called "the springs of Jerusalem"

APPENDIX Friday Sermon[1]

أشهد أن لا إله إلا الله
وأشهد أن محمدا رسول الله

الحمد لله الحمد لله
الحمد لله رب العالمين
والصلاة والسلام على سيدنا
وحبيبنا وقرة عيوننا
محمد رسول الله صلى الله عليه
وعلى آله وصحبه وسلم
أما بعد فقال الله سبحانه
وتعالى في كتابه الكريم
بعد أعوذ بالله من الشيطان الرجيم
بسم الله الرحمن الرحيم

161. قُلْ إِنَّنِي هَدَانِي رَبِّي
إِلَى صِرَاطٍ مُسْتَقِيمٍ
دِينًا قِيَمًا مِّلَّةَ إِبْرَاهِيمَ
حَنِيفًا وَمَا كَانَ مِنَ الْمُشْرِكِينَ

---

1. *Khutbah salat al-jumu'ah* given in the *al-Wahid* Mosque of Milan (AH Shaban 20, 1429/August 22, 2008 CE) by 'Abd al-Haqq Ismail Guiderdoni, Director of the Islamic Institute of Advanced Studies.

162. قُلْ إِنَّ صَلَاتِي وَنُسُكِي
وَمَحْيَايَ وَمَمَاتِي لِلَّهِ رَبِّ الْعَالَمِينَ

163. لَا شَرِيكَ لَهُ وَبِذَلِكَ أُمِرْتُ
وَأَنَا أَوَّلُ الْمُسْلِمِينَ

164. قُلْ أَغَيْرَ اللَّهِ أَبْغِي رَبًّا
وَهُوَ رَبُّ كُلِّ شَيْءٍ وَلَا تَكْسِبُ
كُلُّ نَفْسٍ إِلَّا عَلَيْهَا وَلَا تَزِرُ وَازِرَةٌ
وِزْرَ أُخْرَى ثَمَّ إِلَى رَبِّكُم
مَّرْجِعُكُمْ فَيُنَبِّئُكُم بِمَا كُنتُمْ فِيهِ تَخْتَلِفُونَ

165. وَهُوَ الَّذِي جَعَلَكُمْ خَلَائِفَ
الْأَرْضِ وَرَفَعَ بَعْضَكُمْ فَوْقَ بَعْضٍ
دَرَجَاتٍ لِّيَبْلُوَكُمْ فِي مَا آتَاكُمْ
إِنَّ رَبَّكَ سَرِيعُ الْعِقَابِ
وَإِنَّهُ لَغَفُورٌ رَّحِيمٌ

صدق الله العظيم

68

I testify that there is no god but God and that Muhammad is the messenger of God.

Praise be to God, Praise be to God, Praise be to God, the Cherisher and Sustainer of the Worlds, and Grace and Peace be upon our Master, our Beloved, and the Joy of our Eyes. Muhammad the messenger of God, may God bless him, his family, and his companions and may He grant them peace.

Dear Brothers and Sisters, in *Surat Al-An'am*, "The Cattle," the sixth chapter of the Holy Qur'an, *ayat* 161–65, God the Almighty addresses the Prophet Muhammad—Divine peace and blessing be on him:

Say: "Verily my Lord hath guided me to a straight Way—an upright religion—the cohort of Abraham, the "true in faith," and he "joined not gods with God" (6:161).

Say: "Truly, my prayer and my service of sacrifice, my life and my death, are (all) for God, the Sustainer of the Worlds" (6:162).

No partner hath He: this am I commanded, and I am the first of those who surrender (*muslimin*)" (6:163).

Say: "Shall I seek for (my) Sustainer other than God, when He is the Sustainer of all things (that exist)? Every soul only receives what it deserves (lit. acquires): no bearer of burdens can bear the burden of another. Your goal in the end is towards God: He will tell you the truth of the things wherein ye disputed" (6:164).

"It is He Who hath made you (His) representative followers on the earth: He hath raised you in ranks, some above others: that He may try you in the gifts He hath given you: for thy Lord is quick in punishment: yet He is indeed Oft-forgiving, Most Merciful" (6:165).

Dear Brothers and Sisters, these verses of the Holy Qur'an are some of several passages in which God asks the Prophet to recite a *du'a*, or an invocation using the actual words that He reveals. God expects His Servant, the Prophet, to worship in total submission to the One who is Alone, and there is no better way to worship God than to worship Him with the same words He has chosen to reveal. These invocations from the Qur'an have special importance in the spiritual life of believers who follow the example of the Prophet. This is true also of *Surat al-Ikhlas* (which is said to be symbolically equivalent to one third of the Qur'an), just as it is also true of the two concluding *suwar* (sg. *surah*) known as the verses of protection. These providential invocations are not simply words of worship ordained by God. They are also—because they are words of worship ordained by God—teachings of a spiritual and metaphysical nature. For it is God alone who dispenses the knowledge of Reality, and the Prophet never ceases to ask: "O my Lord, increase my knowledge!"

The invocations that have just been read close the *surah* called The Cattle *(al-An'am)*. They teach us the nature of the "guidance" that God has granted to the Prophet Muhammad by means of the providential descent of the Holy Qur'an, the revelation of Islam. They began with,

> Say: "Verily my Lord hath guided me to a straight Way (*sirat mustaqim*)—an upright religion (*dinan qayyiman*)—the cohort of Abraham (*millat Ibrahim*) the 'true in faith' (*hanifan*), and he 'joined not gods with God' (*wa-ma kana min al-mushrikin*)" (Qur'an 6:161).

In this verse, God uses five expressions, all of which refer to levels of Being, from the metaphysical to the successive stages in sacred history. Islam identifies itself as the right path, the metaphysical axis of the world, crossing and connecting the multiple States of Being. This path allows access to the *supraformal* worlds that are of an intellectual and angelic nature.

Islam renews the axial, or immutable, religion that has been revealed to all Prophets, starting from Adam himself when he repented and God made a pact with him. Islam is linked to the providential adaptation of immutable religion as it was given to Sayyiduna Ibrahim, Abraham. This is when *tawhid*, the affirmation of one God, made all other symbols of the divine attributes disappear like broken idols.

Sayyiduna Ibrahim was the first of a *millah*, or a "cohort," and his descendents were as numerous as the stars in the sky. Among his offspring, the *hunafa'*, or pure believers, preserved the metaphysical transparency of the original message for centuries. They were awaiting a final adjustment, that of Islam, whose metaphysical message is summarized in the *shahadah*. This proclamation of faith insists on *tawhid*, denying any associations with God: *la ilaha illa Allah wahda-Hu la sharika la-Hu*. Like Sayyiduna Ibrahim, and following his example, the Prophet Muhammad refused to accept any "thing that could be associated with God (*shirk*)," breaking idols when he returned to Mecca. However, he placed a protective hand on the holy icon of Sayyidatuna Maryam (Mary).[2] These steps are all providential adaptations of the divine message that was designed to counter the downward march of time. Grace upon grace five times over. *Nur 'ala nur*, "Light on light," issuing forth from the great abundant loving care of God for humanity.

It is very important to understand that the right metaphysical Path, and the primordial Tradition that constitutes its formally revealed expression, are not to be looked for in a hypothetical essence, nor in an even more hypothetical "quintessence" located somewhere above the revealed religions. There is not a "transcendent unity" of religions that can be extracted, or abstracted, from forms. There does not exist an "eternal wisdom," or a *sophia perennis*, independent of the messages of the Prophets that would be sufficient to study in these so-called "post-Prophetic" times in order to inherit knowledge.

On the contrary, metaphysical truth is "framed" or even "incarnated" within the bosom of the revealed religions. The religions themselves are symbolically incarnated five times according the teaching of this verse. Truth is not knowledge that one might be able to derive from the letter of the religions; the text would then be reduced to a lifeless corpse. Truth is the very life of religious forms. Without forms, nothing can be grasped. We cannot leave the times of the Prophets, because these are the very substance of time. We must never forget that we are waiting for the return of a Prophet, Sayyiduna 'Isa (Jesus).

This was also the true message of our Master Shaykh 'Abd al-Wahid Yahya. Unfortunately the message was betrayed again and again by those who believed that the spirit could be grasped without the letter, just as it has been betrayed by those who have forgotten that the letter kills if it is not given life by the spirit. May God help us to continue to be *hunafa'*, pure believers who preserve the purity of Islam as revealed to the Prophet and transmitted through the *silsilah* (chain of transmission) of our Masters up to the present guidance of Shaykh 'Abd al-Wahid and Shaykh Yahya.

---

2. Al-Azraqi, *Akhbar Makkah wa-ma ja'a fi-ha min al-athar*, p. 61. See also, Ibn Ishaq, *Sirat Rasul Allah*, translated by A. Guillaume, *The Life of Muhammad* (Oxford: Oxford University Press, 1982, 7th ed), p. 552, 774.

Following the first invocation at the conclusion of the Chapter of the Cattle (*surat al-An'am*), God explains Islam to His Prophet through the carrying out of *shahadah* and the destruction of idols:

> Say: "Truly, my prayer and my service of sacrifice, my life and my death, are (all) for God, the Sustainer of the Worlds" (Qur'an 6:162). No partner hath He: this am I commanded, and I am the first of those who surrender (*muslimin*)" (Qur'an 6:163).

These verses point us toward understanding that to be truly subject to God is to do all things for the one God, without associating anything with God. When praying and performing ritual acts, every action must acquire the value of a ritual devoted solely to God; life as a whole and death itself (as the ultimate reunion of a human act and an act of God) must both belong to the Lord. Thus we make the real sacrifice to offer what we do to the Lord.

The acts must not be done in our own name but for the name of God—or more accurately, "with," "by," and "in" the name of God. The acts have no value in themselves because, in the words of the *hadith*,[3] they are only intentions—even if intentions without acts are not acts, since they are just intentions. And intention is the will to go towards God and to understand the knowledge given by God.

> Say: "Shall I seek for (my) Sustainer other than God, when He is the Sustainer of all things (that exist)?" (Qur'an 6:164)

This reminds us to reject superficial dichotomies: the sacred world versus the secular world, the modern world versus the traditional world, and the community versus the individual. There is only a secular point of view, a modern point of view, and an individual point of view, which represent just so many errors of perspective regarding the knowledge of reality.

These errors of perspective consist of the belief that we are the real authors, owners, and beneficiaries of all our acts, including the acts of ritual that we perform; this is *shirk*, the most subtle of associations. "The ego" is the worst of idols, as God reminds us in these quoted verses:

---

3. The Prophet said, "Actions are by intentions" (*Sahih Muslim* and *Sahih Bukhari*).

> Every soul (*nafs*) receives (lit. acquires) only what it deserves: no bearer of burdens can bear the burden of another (Qur'an 6:164).

> Or, more precisely, echoing the words of one of the last verses of *Surah al-Baqarah*, the Chapter of The Cow: "The soul shall have that which it acquires and owe that which it seeks to acquire for itself" (Qur'an 2:286). Being subject to God and following the example of the Prophet is to approach God, offering to Him all of our acts done in His name, as the sole origin and the sole purpose of our life on Earth: Say: "Truly, my prayer and my service of sacrifice, my life and my death, are (all) for God, the Sustainer of the Worlds" (Qur'an 6:162).

But we must understand that sacrifice, in the literal and etymological meaning of the word, means "making sacred" by offering something to God. Sacrifice makes God the origin and purpose of our lives; it is not a passive process. It is inseparable from a sense of responsibility. This responsibility derives from the fact that we will be asked to account for our acts and recognize whether we were really searching for God in doing what we did: "No soul shall bear the burden of another." We are responsible because we will have to answer this question about the true intentions of our actions on the Day of Judgment. God warns us: "Your return will be to your Lord, and he will then inform you about what you were in disagreement." May God help us carry out all the ritual, community-based, familial, and professional acts of our life in order to seek His face, which dwells alone. This is the only way that each one of us will be a worthy vicegerent, or a *khalifa* (of God) on Earth (*khala'if al-'ard*) (6:165). As *khalifas*, etymologically we will be "representative followers" of God and not *mukhtalifun* (divergents) (6:164) who only follow their "ego." Consequently, in following God we unite in Him, as opposed to following our individual impulses and subsequently breaking up into the multiplicity of possibilities.

Dear Brothers and Sisters, our blessed community has the responsibility to bear witness to faith and knowledge in this world where God has bestowed those qualities. Our testimony is the *shahadah* and the metaphysical principles of primordial Tradition. These principles were providentially adapted by both the exoteric and esoteric Islamic forms, then reflected in every sphere of life through all the means that God has put at our disposal in contingent ways and circumstances. Our responsibility only makes sense if we realize—in the initiatory sense of the term, meaning in the sense of *tahqiq* (spiritual realization)—that it is God who testifies through us when we pronounce the *shahadah*. This is the special responsibility that God has entrusted to us. It is a responsibility impossible to bear with our own forces, but which raises us up if we entrust ourselves to the hands of God. For if the servant takes one step towards God, God takes ninety-nine steps toward him.

God says in a verse of the Holy Qur'an: "He has raised some of you in differing degrees above the others, to test you with his gifts" (Qur'an 6:165). These higher degrees refer to the initiatory hierarchies of *ihsan* (conscious worship). The Prophet described *ihsan* as worshipping God "as if we saw God; and if we do not see Him, He sees us." May God elevate us by degrees (*darajat)*, and bring us closer to Him, so that we may be worthy of this gift that we have inherited: the Muhammadan *barakah* (grace), transmitted to Shaykh Ahmad ibn Idris al-Fasi through Sayyiduna al-Khadir, the ever-alive "green" prophet who met Sayyiduna Musa (Moses),[4] and then the Masters of the Path up to Shaykh 'Abd ar-Rashid al-Linki and our dearly-beloved Masters Shaykh 'Abd al-Wahid and Shaykh Yahya.

May God help us keep the remembrance of His name, whose flashing lights enwrapped us last night. May God help us preserve the memory of our Master, Shaykh 'Abd al-Wahid Yahya René Guénon, for the living and lived understanding of metaphysical doctrine. May God support our blessed community and each one of its members in the face of constant hardships, endowing us with this holy *sabr* (patience) that is required of believers in these times. This we are taught by Surat *al-'Asr*, which our younger brothers and sisters have learned recently. Such patience is essential to fulfilling the purpose of initiatory hierarchies: the general purpose is to do the will of God, and in particular to test those to whom He has made the gift of nearness, testing them precisely through this gift itself. Those most tested are the Prophets, then the Saints, then the initiated according to the level at which God has placed them. Last come all the rest of the believers according to their degree of faith. This test is the measure of the knowledge that we must take from the world: knowledge that deepens our understanding of the meaning of the *shahadah*, bearing witness to the fact that there is no deity

---

4. Qur'an, 18:65-82.

74

but God and that Muhammad is the messenger of God, *la ilaha illa Allah Muhammadun rasul Allah*. Thus we may arrive at the goal of this life before the hereafter—*fi 'd-dunya qabla al-akhirati*. As our *wird* (litany) says: we must live in a real way, "in every glance and in every breath, everyone always containing the knowledge of God."

Among the hardships that we face, there is not just the recently growing misunderstanding and hostility between men and women against the Truth that compels us to find ways of adapting our witness to eschatological circumstances. More importantly, we must face the hardships presented by the deviations and falsifications that we discover on the many journeys and visits to which God has directed us as part of our testimony (*al-balagh*) and our test (*al-bala'*).

We must give thanks to God for His help in preserving what makes us a true *tariqah*: exoteric and esoteric doctrinal orthodoxy (preserved through our adherence to the metaphysical message of primordial Tradition in its Islamic adaptation); exoteric and esoteric orthopraxy (preserved through the *barakah*'s regular transmission along a known *silsilah* going back to the Prophet); integration into a community of brothers while simultaneously anticipating the eschatological meeting of religions at the end of time; and, finally, we must give thanks to God for enabling us to do His Will and seek His face only.

There is a correspondence between these five elements and the five pillars of Islam: doctrinal orthodoxy is related to understanding the *shahadah*; orthopraxy and regular transmission are related to prayer in the *qiblah,* which binds us to the Centre; the community is connected to the *zakat* (public alms-giving), which purifies us; openness towards the eschatological convergence of religions evokes the *hajj*'s significance as anticipation of the meeting on the Day of Judgment; and, finally, the desire for God alone relates to the *siyam*, or the fast of Ramadan. God says in a *hadith qudsi*: "Everything that the son of Adam does belongs to him, except fasting; because it is for Me, and I [alone] reward it."[5] Alas, it seems very clear that many of today's *turuq* in both the West and the East lack one or more of these five elements, especially the awareness of the eschatological expectation of Sayyiduna 'Isa (Jesus) and the desire to know God alone.

---

5. *Kullu 'amal ibn Adam lahu illa al-sawm fa-innahu li wa-ana ajzi bihi* (*Sahih Bukhari*).

God expects us to bear that special burden. That is our purpose, from which all our actions proceed, because the message of the primordial Tradition will manifest through Christ one last time at the end of this present cycle of time. If we ask, "Why us?" then we must understand that the *hawariyyun* (apostles) asked the same question when they were chosen by Sayyiduna 'Isa. This is a grace of God, who can see inside hearts. May God help us to be worthy of such grace during the Ramadan fast,which begins in a few days, *insha'Allah* (God willing). May He help us be worthy of the grace that renews our desire to look for His face only, His face which endures while all else is fleeting and quickly fading.

Amin.